The 6 Figure Cleaning Business Master Class Manual

Compilation of Class Materials, Previous Ebook Material, Cleaning Proposal Sample, How to Calculate Price, & More!

By Victoria Amador

What's Included?

INTRODUCTION – WHO IS THIS MATERIAL DESIGNED FOR?

This manual includes all my knowledge on how to start and grow a million-dollar cleaning company in a short amount of time. This is not for lazy people looking to make a quick buck. This is for serious cleaning business owner ready to grow their companies to millions of dollars. Here I include all the information I provide on my video course found at

http://tremendouslife.com/the-6-figure-cleaning-company-master-class

called The 6 Figure Cleaning Business Master Class which is a video class explaining in detail all the content you'll see in the screenshots throughout this manual. I have also included all the content from my previous ebook where I discuss all the lessons I have learned throughout the years at starting a cleaning company with no money to earning over a million within 6 years.

Disclaimer: I am not a writer so you'll probably notice lots of grammatical errors and sentence composition issues so this book is not for those looking to read a book for pleasure – *THIS is a manual with lots of material that are not meant to flow like a book….this is FOR THOSE READY TO TAKE ACTION AND APPLY WHAT WE DISCUSS HERE TO EARN MONEY strategically and consistently.*

What's included:

- *Over 70% of all the materials provided in the cleaning business master class available on tremendouslife.com,*
- *How to start a cleaning business*
- *Cleaning proposal / quote sample*
- *Websites mistakes and lessons learned*
- *Getting your first customers*
- *Direct marketing can be a waste of time*

- *Operational procedures*

- *Advice to hire your first employees*

- *SWOT analysis*

- *How to calculate pricing for your accounts*

- *How to fire employees and clients*

- *Marketing tips to earn over 6 figures*

- *Process mapping to improve your cleaning business*

- *Google listing tips*

- *Customer service templates from asking for feedback to asking for payment for services rendered*

- *Email marketing samples*

- *How to ask for payments consistently with our templates*

- *Telephone questionnaire*

- *Screenshots of excel files from the class (if you want the actual excel file with forecasting and HR tools the only way is to purchase the video class)*

- *And much more!*

Visit tremendouslife.com to get an idea on what the actual course is all about or just read this book —either way you'll be ahead of most 99% of all others thinking or already owning a cleaning business. I have friends that have been in the cleaning business for 10 years and still have not achieve revenues over a half million...reasons are many but the number one reason I've noticed is that they have not systems in place. You can run a successful company without proper systems and yes you do need a system for everything even for ordering supplies, answering the phone, responding to emails, your sales and marketing, training and human resources system to even how you dress (uniforms), speak to your clients and much more!

So the first part of the manual I'll go over what we learned in the previous book called Real Stories, Lessons & Tips from Someone Who Started a Cleaning Company and Grew Revenues to over a million in 6 years". And then I'll go into all the information we shared with the video course buyers so you'll have the same info (most of it) and you will be able to use this to start and grow your cleaning service.

So let's start!

In my previous ebook, I discussed how easy is getting into the cleaning industry. In most states you do not need special licenses or permits. All you need is basic insurance to protect yourself and your clients, cleaning supplies, and a good amount of processes and marketing technique. You will make mistakes and learn from them, but really it doesn't take a rocket scientist. A lot of immigrants get into the cleaning business because really you do not even need to be fluent in English to make good money in the industry. Of course, it will be a huge help if you are fluent in English, but I have seen business owners making six figures that are not fluent in English. They often hire freelancers and employees that do speak proper English for website development, marketing copy, and even for their sales force. The key is to be consistent and methodical about your operational and marketing efforts. You do not need to buy a franchise to be successful in the cleaning industry. You can start small and hire as your business grows.

I wrote the ebook to help you think about how to start and run your cleaning company by avoiding the mistakes I've already made. So let's start with what resources are available to you for free today so you can start getting an idea of the challenges and opportunities cleaning business owners face. A lot of the LinkedIn business owners log in to ask for idea on how to price (which will cover in this book as well), how to hire, how to fire both customers and employees, and a lot more. Join some of these groups so you can start your journey today! There are several industry sources that I found to be extremely helpful in my understanding of commercial business. Within a couple of weeks of starting the residential division, I found LinkedIn groups that offer support to business owners. The most constructive group that provided much insight was the Association of Residential Cleaning Services, International also known as ARCSI. I highly recommend registering as a member if you are not a member already. Soon after I found more groups that become a huge help for getting answers on daily questions I had while getting the business off ground. Below is a list of other resources I found helpful.

ISSA-The Worldwide Cleaning Industry Association

MarketingProfs

Business Growth for the Commercial Cleaning Industry

Global Cleaning / Janitorial Group

Cleaning Industry Research Institute

IEHA - Uniting Facility Managers Worldwide

NBSC Group

Cleaning Services

ARCSI, A Division of ISSA

Home Cleaner Magazine

Rags to Riches Cleaning Resource

Professional Housekeeping

MarketingProfs PRO

Building Service Contractors Association International (BSCAI) CleaningBusinessToday.com

Cleaning Industry News

MyHouseCleaningBiz.com

TheJanitorialStore.com

These websites have info on how to set up forms, train customer service employees, conduct walkthroughs, and price services. They also have recorded talks with other businesses and an online forum for members to discuss challenges. I highly recommend taking a look at their sites. If you are in the residential cleaning then join myhousecleaningbiz.com, and if you are more into commercial then join thejanitorialstore.com – and if you are both, then I would highly recommend joining both sites, because every dollar I invested in their paid-member site saved me a lot of headache, time, and potential employee or client issues. When I have a major challenge or project, I jump on those sites and go through the member's library to see if I can find solutions or ideas in that area. I just love their sites so much!

I also found all the cleaning industry related groups to be quite useful. The list above is all of all the free groups I belong to that I think you should at least check out. I belong to other groups unrelated to the cleaning industry that I listed above and I believe that as a cleaning business owner you should check out these groups. MarketingProfs.com is an amazing marketing site that includes free webinars! I have been a member of MarketingProfs.com since 2012 and I keep paying because I believe that they really opened me up to digital marketing and we would not have thrived the way we have without the ideas I got from taking their classes and reading their reports and content!

When it was time for me to get going in the commercial division, NBSC Group with Michael Breitzke really helped me with a commercial proposal template, pricing strategies, and so much more. You should definitely find Michael and at least chat with him and see if there is a good reason for you to join the NBSC Group.

The first year I also purchased a few training programs from Rags to Riches – they saved me thousands and thousands of dollars in training. If you are new or already in business and do not have your cleaners in a good training program I would highly (and very seriously) suggest that you purchase Sharon's training at successmaideasy.com – it's seriously worth every single penny. The training program Sharon has is truly amazing.

Michael Champion has a great podcast "Grow My Cleaning Company". I just found him in 2016 and got hooked. I watched many of his podcasts and know that his info is worth your time. His podcast covers everything from how to market your cleaning company guerrilla style to how to prepare for your exit strategy.

There are so many resources out there and cleaning masterminds groups such as those put together by Debbie Sardone, a coach in the cleaning industry and an amazing person who really wants to see the industry move forward and convey a truly professional appearance in everything we do. She has done it all from consultancy, speaker, author and still owns her cleaning company and put together the Cleaning for a Reason organization that is so well known in our industry which serves women cancer patients with free house cleaning from cleaning companies that sign up to receive such service.

Because of all the online and offline groups and programs I have participated in, I was inspired to create an organization that works with our employees to treat employees properly and inspire them to achieve their dreams. I fell in love with the industry by better understanding that this is a huge industry where billions of dollars are spent every year in keeping our world safe from illnesses. Actually, the latest IbisWorld Report indicates that 56 billion dollars are spent worldwide in cleaning services. Being in the cleaning industry is hard both emotionally because if you are a professional and now have to learn to clean it can be challenging for you to feel comfortable with being a highly paid cleaner. Many professionals from other countries when they first arrive to the USA they also have a big problem with this. We had hired doctors, professors, lawyers and now they are cleaning homes and buildings and it really becomes a big issue for them initially especially if the clients are not very respectful to them. The industry is also hard on you physically because obviously it's a go-go business when things are always happening, you are either cleaning, training, inspection or doing walkthroughs in your cleaning business. If you decide to join the industry, take time to look at the bigger picture. Just because anyone can start with a broom and mop does not mean you should operate the same way. One of your key differentiators could be that image of professionalism that you can bring into the market. Most cleaning business operators are cleaning by themselves according to IbisWorld Industry Report 56172. In the Ibis report which may no longer be active since the report is updated every few years and its quite expensive so I do not recommend buying it, it is indicated that industry operators often face price-based competition. I can testify to this; the competition is truly like an African jungle where the bigger and stronger often win the large clients, so we had to find ways to compete on a different level.

(https://www.ibisworld.com/industry-trends/market-research-reports/)

Side note: Our cleaning industry NAICS code is 56172 so whenever you need to do your taxes or look for an industry report make sure to use that code.

Chapter 1 Quick Review on How to Start a Cleaning Company

Prior to incorporating – figure out who will be your partners –if you are going at it alone –I recommend you get a business minded friend to bounce off ideas. If you are going to have partners decide now how is the ownership divided. It will be much better for everyone to know what's in it for them. You may want to hire a lawyer to create a partnership agreement with all the rules of what would happen if you or one of your partners leave the business, or if someone goes on disability or if someone is married and divorces, etc. All these things your attorney will help you figure out but perhaps you should wait to do that until you are earning money to pay your attorney! Also figure out how much each of you will put down as an investment to start your new cleaning company and how would that affect your ownership percentages.

Deciding on a business entity is a big decision and you should discuss options with your accountant and attorney. You have to worry about tax savings and asset protection. This is only a general review and you must consult your accountant and attorney as I do not have a background in those areas. Here is an overview of some possible ways to legally recognize your business.

A Sole Proprietor: is a basic business entity. Mostly for individuals doing business under their own names and collecting a check made out to their name. You deposit checks to your personal account and pay expenses from the same account. This is dangerous for many reasons, but mostly because under a sole proprietorship entity you do not have any liability protection. Therefore, you could be personally liable for any claims against your business. You could reduce the risks by purchasing insurance. You would also be taxed on 100% of profits.
Sole proprietor is good for those that want to start slow and that have minimal exposure to risks.

Filing as an LLC or Corporation may cost more money initially but eventually as you grow and pay taxes these structures can save you money. Once you file to incorporate and get your EIN # - start filing away —make sure you keep good records of all your documents (legal documents, receipts, etc.). Keeping all receipts scanned into a cloud and backup folder on a separate cloud or hard drive. Receipts fade away quickly and you don't know when you may be audited. Once you decide on what type of business entity/structure you want to use then you have to figure out how to name your company. Figuring out what to name your company is probably one of the most important decisions you have to make at this point. Use professional words or create your own but keep it professional.

Side Story about naming your company:

We choose Company xyz as our company legal name and later we thought that we wanted to add an s to Maid portion of the name —because we had websites, all legal documents, all brochure, business cards etc. all advertising documents under Company xyz —the cost to change it just to add an S didn't seem worth it to us so instead we bought an extra domain tremendousmaids.com and forward it to tremendousmaid.com —but all of our emails are all with tremendousmaid.com —the biggest challenge is dealing with the emails —if we change it we have to pay more to run 2 emails with the s and one without the s to be save —over a period of time this is extremely expensive. So, the lesson here is to pick your name carefully and thoughtfully to avoid making the same mistake.

Side Note: You can always change your company's structure later and pay for the changes depending on what they may be. Don't feel like you are stuck with one company structure for the rest of your life because that's not the case at all.

It's hard to organize a book to help someone get started in any business. So many things have to happen almost simultaneously so after a lot of consideration I decided for the first major piece of advice to be related to putting your thoughts down on paper in the form of a short version business plan. So this next session, let's focus on what you should think about before starting your business. And even if you already filed with your secretary of state and applied for an EIN # and have started operating your business, you should still do a short version if you did not do it before.

CHAPTER 2 - A SHORT BUSINESS PLAN CAN SAVE YOU LOTS OF HEADACHES

A business plan will give you a better idea of what is it you want to do it and why. So let's take a few minutes to discuss why a business plan is important. You do not need a 30-pages business plan. However, it would be highly beneficial to have a short version of a business plan with the major sessions, what would you do, what would you offer to your clients, why would they buy from you, how much would it cost, how would you finance the business, a financial forecast for first 1-3 years, and how would you get customers.

The reality is that a long term business plan is good for you to dream —most business plans are not realistic at all and over the years I have looked at my business plans and laughed. If you are going for funding and want to get investors, create a business plan that gets you what you need while still being slightly conservative but don't over promise because it will be harder than you think. If you are one of the luckiest person who meet their numbers that's great but this is a new adventure and you don't know what you will find in the market until you start.

Because you can find plenty of business plans out there for free and perhaps better than my business plans, I am not going over that here but what I am including is a few key tips/advice/lessons that helped me go over $100k the first year in operations. And If you follow the tips here, I am 100% confident you can do more than half a million within 3 years of operations. Just so you know, in the residential cleaning world on average small companies unless they are franchise they take all their life-times trying to get to half a million. Unless you have the money to buy and operate a franchise, I highly recommend taking notes, using the tips here and visiting all the LinkedIn groups to get immersed in the cleaning world. The key to success is in applying what you learn immediately and consistently.

To get you thinking big, let's do this quick exercise below to help you get going with your business plan:

Think about why you want to start this business. What's the vision you have for your cleaning company? Close your eyes and imagine if everything was absolutely perfect and you had a million dollars to start your cleaning business, what would your business look like? Your mission and vision can have a significant impact on your outreach to local non-profits, media, and even when you get ready to get a loan from the bank if done right. Also consider the key risks you would be taking by starting your business and decide if it's worth the risk. You can make money with this type of business, but you will also need to put in some serious hours.

Initially, I worked 14-16 hours-days for years until I decided that I also needed to be a good mom and started taking weekends. I have a friend that started his business right after high school with no idea of how to even clean a window. He decided to work only on commercial accounts and limit the client list so he could go out and party and have fun. His business did over 100k in sales the first year just with commercial cleaning and subcontracted out the work. He would acquire the accounts, do some management, and have everything else done by his two reliable subcontractors. That plan worked for him, but I did things very different. I wanted to control operations, client experience, employee relations, and everything in between, so I worked really hard to set up a residential and commercial cleaning company to grow and grow tremendously. My friend on the other hand was more interested in hiring sub-contractors, having them do the work and he would take a bigger portion by paying subcontractors and not paying taxes on these sub-contractors, working from home, not doing a lot of branding for his company so we were completely different in how we ran our companies. He makes more money per job than my company but we are a higher volume company compared to his so think about what structure works best for you and your needs as a business owner.

Before we move onto something else I want to review major lessons I learned with our website. Your website is your first step towards a great professional appearance in your client's mind. It's vital for your success in this cleaning business for your website to be considered as one of your most precious assets.

CHAPTER 3 - WEBSITES 101 KEY LEARNING POINTS BASED ON REAL EXPERIENCE:

Before we paid a lot of attention to our website we put a lot of emphasis on postcards and direct mail. We quickly learned to figure out which advertising medium were working for us because we tracked which advertising platform was working well just by asking the potential clients how did they find us. We spent a lot of capital and human resources on our marketing strategy. Some worked and some did not. I wish I had known some things when it came to advertising back in 2011; I had to learn the hard way.

Tip #1: One of the most important things you will own in your business is your website – there are tons of blogs, books, and webinars on this so I am only going to suggest that you should hire a professional copy writer to help with your site content. You can find one on upwork.com, but you have to give them good instructions on the tone and voice of your business so the website is an extension of you and your team. They need your ideas and rough drafts so they can make whatever you give them better. They cannot do magic because they really don't know what and how you would do your business so don't let them do all the work. This is actually a great way for you to figure out really on what basis you will be competing and acquiring clients. For example, what's your main differentiation factor? For us at Company xyz, it is all about the 5 Star Hotel Cleaning because the founders had many years of luxury hotel and resort experience. For us we were selling on the promise that our customers would feel pampered in their own homes because we're are going to provide them with a five-star cleaning experience. We knew that we could truly deliver on that promise and so it became the cornerstone of every piece of marketing material from uniforms to how soon the phone is answered and how we manage our customer feedback and complaints.

Tip #2: Your website must have a clear differentiation strategy of why, how, and what is it that you do. Obviously, you need a clear call to action whether it's "call us now at xxxxxxx" or a "request a quote" page or an online "book now" page. Whatever it is, make sure it's easy to find from your home page, and any other pages. You can take a look at tremendousmaid.com to get an idea. Make sure you do not copy content from other cleaning companies. Google will know and it will penalize your website. Visit different cleaning company's pages, pick the items you like the most and note the items you like the least, and then go off to develop your own content. If you simply copy and paste, your site won't have any personality and clients will notice.

Something important to consider in your website is how you want your company to be perceived. How will the copy convey your image, and how will your clients feel and think when they see your name? What words and sentences bet convey those thoughts?

Tip #3: Customize your website's visual content, or pay a photographer to shoot really good photos & videos. A photo session can be just $500 dollars and you can have all the photos you need to use good images instead of stock photos. Some research indicates that stock photos can hurt your website because clients are sophisticated, and can tell that you are using stock photos. Spending a few hundred dollars for professional visual content can be truly worth it. When you do your photo shoot, use a nice home. If you don't have one available, rent one via Airbnb for less than $200, This way, you can have a place that's nice where you and your team can go to take amazing photos that can be used for years. Prior to scheduling your photo shoot, make sure to have your uniforms and the right cleaning equipment and supplies. If you are up to it, you can even offer someone with a nice place to clean their space for free in exchange for letting your photographer take photos and even a video of how the cleaning is being done.

Now I want to go over how to get your first few customers. Actually if you do this right, this can generate dozens of new regular weekly, biweekly or monthly clients for your company.

CHAPTER 4 - GETTING YOUR FIRST CUSTOMERS

The first two months after starting my business, nothing happened. I was getting really nervous. I kept thinking that I had failed. I kept thinking that everyone who had told me I was making a mistake was right. Some days I felt like someone must have done some voodoo on me because nothing was making sense. Eventually, I decided that if regular print advertising was not working, we needed to discount the service so we could get our first testimonials and reviews online and hopefully some traffic to our website. So we did. At that time, there was a local company doing online coupons similar to Groupon and we tried them. We sold a few hundred coupons for $39 per cleaning and then did another one within the same month with Weforia and after selling over 400 coupons the phones started ringing. It was March when things really picked up for us. We were working six days per week. The craziest thing we did was to go clean a home 2 hours from us to fulfill a coupon in hopes of getting positive reviews, and we did. Because we didn't initially have other regular customers we were able to fulfill the Groupon callers any day or time. On one occasion, not only did we drive 1.5 hours away in another state but the client requested the cleaning to be done before 9am for an open house so we drove to New Hampshire from Boston at 4am and finished just 5 minutes before the open house. She didn't have a coupon, so we charged a total of $125 for over 3 hours of work with 3 cleaners. The service was discounted, but that's what it took for us to get our first few 5 star reviews on yelp. From them we started getting quote requests and phone calls inquiring about regular service. Some of the coupon holders also became regular clients. But overall, most coupon holders only wanted the cleaning because of the discount they were getting. The coupon holders' homes were also the most difficult to clean since most were in very bad shape. But again, it was the best way for us because we didn't have the funds to do any other type of advertising.

Major Tip – Be Careful: If you consider doing coupons such as Groupon or LivingSocial or anything similar, make sure you have a strategy in place. Indicate to the coupon company that you will only sell x amount and provide clear instructions of how the coupons can be used and on what days or times. Coupon buyers are famous for asking for too much, even though they know they got a really great deal. For example, if you decide to sell 200 coupons, how many of them can you fulfill without harming your brand's reputation? How many homes can you clean per day? How many days until you clean for your regular customers and new coupon buyers? What restrictions can you indicate to cover yourself from potentially creating a nightmare? I know of companies that have gone out of business after selling coupons because they couldn't fulfill their sales. It's dangerous to sell thinking you will break even. When you sell a coupon, you have to discount the price normally by a lot, maybe 50% or more so a company like Groupon would be interested in featuring you. Then, from the half you sell, you have to give the coupon distributer a percentage of each sale, then you have to cover payroll, cleaning supplies, etc. to provide the service so at the end of the day you probably lost money.

Depending on your finances, you may want to pay the minimum fee to get on Yelp ads. Yelp was the most effective advertising piece for us at Company xyz initially. We started paying the minimum fee of $325 or so per month in 2011. Once we started, over 90% of the calls we received were coming from Yelp. Because we relied so heavily on Yelp we also noticed a huge drop in call volume or quote requests when we had a bad review. So, for my first two years, there were times when I would get up at 2am to check Yelp because if there was a bad review, I knew sales could go down as much as 25% which is a big deal for a tiny little company. A side note when responding to negative Yelp reviews is to ensure you are always very diplomatic. Do not be negative towards your customers, keep it highly professional and if at all possible try to reach the customer to rectify the problem before responding online. If you rectify the customer ask them to update/edit or remove the negative complaint.

Make sure to diversify your advertising. We tried a local newspaper for 2 towns that yielded the highest return on investment even more so than Yelp. Basically, for each $1 we invested in this local newspaper, (called the Suburban Shopper) we got a return of $3, but we could only attract a handful of clients per every 3 quarters or so. It was highly effective but very small number of clients were obtained since the newspaper was only sent to 2 towns. So, we put the majority of our marketing online using platforms such as Yelp, Google Adwords, website maintenance / updates, social media, and email marketing. Out of all of them the two that worked best for us were Google SEO and advertising on Yelp the first year or so. Email marketing started to work really well after we had lots of successful with Google & Yelp. Nowadays, everything is automatic when it comes to our sales efforts, there is a clear process in place and the entire team knows which part is their responsibility.

As I mentioned before, although Getting Your First Customers is vital, I would say it is just as important to know what to do and how to provide the service to the customer. So before you start booking clients, think about how would the phone be answer when someone calls to inquire about your service, how would you respond to emails if the inquiry comes thru your website. When would the client be invoiced? Are you demanding payment the day of service or are you allowing the clients a 3-days grace period? For example, for residential clients we require payment upon service delivery but some clients do take a little longer so we have to a process on how to follow up to receive payment for services rendered. So for me, lesson #3 on Operational Procedures is super important for successful growth of your cleaning company. But before we got to lesson #4 on Operational Procedures lets also discuss on lesson #2 why we failed with postcards and then on lesson #3 we will discuss how to maximize your website by having a great sign up on your site for enewsletter marketing. I think all of this almost comes before operations just so your website and advertising to get your first customers start on the right path to success.

Don't forget to install Google Analytics ---it will help you determine if your website is working or not and give you insights into what needs to be changed.

Google Analytics Month / Year	Sessions	User	% New Sessions	Returning Visito	Pageviews	Pages per Session	Avg Session Tim	Bounce Rate
	Convertion %	14%						
Nov Overview								
Nov-11	120	68	56.67%	43.30%	269	2.24	7:38	65.83%
Nov-12	568	355	58%	42%	2039	3.59	4:28	37.85%
Nov-13	439	348	73%	27.70%	1044	2.38	1:42	52.62%
Nov-14	868	795	0.886	0.114	1493	1.72	0.052777778	0.7408
Nov-15	891	692	0.7407	0.2593	1598	1.79	0.059722222	0.7003
AVG Convertion Rates	547.5	70%						
New Sessions #	383.62							
Convertion %	12%							
Dec Overview								
Dec-11	322	215	64%	36%	538	1.67	2:46	72.98%
Dec-12	581	356	56.28%	43.40%	1976	3.4	4:10	41.65%
Dec-13	390	302	72.31%	27.70%	1034	2.65	2:08	42.31%
Dec-14	468	385	0.7671	0.2329	933	1.99	0.074305556	0.6282
Dec-15	0	0	0	0	0	0	0	0
AVG Convertion Rates	260.75	54%						
New Sessions #	140.44							
Convertion %	33%							

Figure 2 Track everything including Google Analytics

Chapter 5 - Why we failed with postcards advertising

The first thing we did was put together double sided flyers in heavy stock size 4x9". Because we didn't have a lot of cash, we decided to have a graphic designer design and print the flyers, and we would deliver the flyers to homes in certain towns that had the high income we needed. Everything was fine and 6 of us (my family, not employees) spent an entire weekend delivering flyers and putting them in mailboxes in 3 towns. It was hard work and on Monday we received a call from the post offices from the different towns telling us that all the flyers would be removed if we didn't pick them up that day. It was impossible to pick all those flyers from the mailboxes, so most of them ended up in the trash. The main lesson I learned is that somethings when you think you are saving money you are just throwing money away. Make sure to understand what you can and cannot put in client's homes. Door hangers are a safe way because you simply hang it on clients' doors but if there are gates you could be crossing the line so make sure you know the local law before entering a potential client's premise.

Next, we decided to do 40k postcards in a packet that went out with 25 other businesses (no other cleaning company was in the packet). Our business was 1 of the 25 or so on the postcards in with other architects, designers, painting companies, pool services, and other entertainment installation services. We agreed to do it for 2 years, and at the end of the 2 years about 360,000 postcards had been delivered and we only acquired about a dozen or so clients. Not worth the investment. But we were new, and perhaps did not have a good enough incentive for clients to call us or perhaps it was the fact that the postcard was delivered with 25 other cards. The major lesson I learned with these postcards is that pretty well designed cards does not equal to the phone ringing. Make sure your offer is clear, you must have a clear call to action that speaks to the potential buyer. Most of the recipients were in towns and I found out the hard way that most of the residents in some of this towns with huge mansions preferred to hire their own maids so they can do laundry, cooking, pick up kids from day care / school so not our main target market.

Anyway, we quickly realized that advertising on yelp and focusing on Google organic search was much more valuable. It was simply to figure out what was and was not working because we asked all clients how they found us. Yelp and Google were the top sources of lead generation so we put more efforts into Yelp and blogging to rank higher on Google. We then also discovered email marketing and fell in love with marketing automation. I wrote a quick e-book (Triple your Revenues with Marketing Automation for Your Cleaning Company available on amazon but for the most part everything you need to know is also included in this book).

CHAPTER 6 - HOW TO TAKE ADVANTAGE OF YOUR CLIENT LIST?

Having a social media plan has been good to reinforce our brand but only a handful of clients have come to us after having us thru Facebook or twitter. If I had to do only 1 I would focus on organic search strategies / creation while you start obtaining emails and names for your newsletters and email marketing simultaneously.

Why email marketing? According to Outbound Engine – a very well-known site indicates:

1. Email marketing averages an ROI of $38 for every $1 spent. (DMA National Client Email Report 2015)

2. For 89 percent of marketers, email serves as the primary channel for lead generation. (Mailigen)

3. Email has become the top source of analytics data for marketing professionals, with 41 percent relying on performance data. (Forbes)

4. For one in five companies, email marketing provides an ROI greater than 70-to-1. (DMA National Client Email Report 2015)

Source: https://www.outboundengine.com/blog/20-shocking-email-marketing-stats-business-owners-know/

Email marketing can help you tremendously if you use it wisely. Below is a sample of the type of content you could create for your email campaigns.

Figure 3 Sample of Digital Marketing Content Plan

| Decision Stage | Content Grid | | | | Segments | |
	Subject	Format	Question it Answers	Delivery Date	Strategic Partners	Professiona Offices
Awareness						
	Property Manager Case Study	Case Study			x	x
	Law Office Case Study	Case Study			x	x
	Investment vs Expense 5/5 Series	Ebook			x	x
	Real Estate Lunch and ILearn	Event				x
	Holiday News Letter	Newsletter		Major Holidays	x	x
	Avoiding Sick Days	Whitepaper			x	x
	Avoiding Seasonal Illness	Whitepaper			x	x
	Identifying Janitorial Needs	Whitepaper			x	x
	Cleaning Business Conference	Webinar			x	x
	Yelp Review	Review			x	x
	2014 BBCC Cleaning Report	Pricing			x	x
Interest						
	How To Choose the Best Janitorial Service for You	Blog				x
	No Substitute for a 5-Star Clean	Blog			x	x
	Increasing Enrollment	Blog				
	How To Choose the Best Janitorial Service for You	Guide/Ebook			x	x
	Choosing the Best Janitorial Service	Whitepaper			x	x
	Identifying Janitorial Needs	Whitepaper			x	x
	Survey Analysis	Infographic			x	x
	2014 BBCC Cleaning Report	Pricing			x	x

Type	Content	Audience	Word Count	Piece
Blog	Investment vs Expense 1/5 Series	Awareness	327	1
Blog	Investment vs Expense 2/5 Series	Awareness	240	1
Blog	Investment vs Expense 3/5 Series	Awareness	274	1
Blog	Investment vs Expense 4/5 Series	Awareness		1
Blog	Investment vs Expense 5/5 Series	Awareness		1
Blog	How To Choose the Best Janitorial Service for You	Interest, Consideration		1
Blog	No Substitute for a 5-Star Clean	Interest, Consideration		1
Blog	Introduction to BBCC Team	Closed		1
Blog	Having an All-Female management	Closed		1
Blog	Helping Migrant Workers	Closed		1
Blog				
Case Study	Property Manager Case Study	Awareness		1
Case Study	Law Office Case Study	Awareness		1
Case Study				
Ebook	Investment vs Expense 5/5 Series	Awareness		1
Ebook	How To Choose the Best Janitorial Service for You	Interest		1
Event	Real Estate Lunch and Learn	Awareness		1
Holiday Greeting	General Greeting	Awareness, Interest, Consideration, Closed		1
Info Graphic	Why BBCC is the best choice	Interest, Consideration		1
News	Monthly Newsletter	Awareness, Interest, Consideration, Closed		1
News				
News				
News				
RFP	RFP	Interest, Consideration		1
RFP				
Seasonal Reminder	Flu Season/Sickness	Interest		1
Video	Short Investment vs Expense	Awareness		1
Video	Management Interviews	Interest, Consideration, Closed		1
White Paper	Avoiding Sick Days	Awareness		1
White Paper	Avoiding Seasonal Illness	Awareness		1
White Paper	Choosing the Best Janitorial Service	Interest		1

Figure 4 Email Campaign Sheet Sample

Marketing automation takes some time and a lot of effort but long term has huge positive impact. Hopefully you have more financial resources than we did and can at least try a handful of different advertising tactics to see what works for you best. Different areas have different demographics and what has worked for us doesn't necessary means it will work for you. The only reason why we know what worked and didn't work is because we tracked everything possible. We always ask how the customer found us and we analyzed the google analytics, yelp analytics daily, weekly, monthly. So from the day you open up your doors start tracking in google sheets or excel everything you possibly can —from how many customers per day you service, time it took per home based on home details such as square feet, # of bedrooms and # of bathrooms etc. —whether it was in suburban area or downtown etc. ---if you don't get a scheduling program platform you should start with google calendar and sheets and within months start researching which scheduling platform is best. You can't run a cleaning business without a good scheduling program platform in place. We used Service Autopilot, scheduling manager by thoughtful systems and tried several others. Initially we had a web based platform but it had some bugs and we wanted something more reliable, we found a platform that promised to do everything we wanted but eventually we realized it was a major mistake mostly because we did not get the web-based version. When you are starting in business and the office is off-site you need constant access to the info so web-based is the way to go. And even when you get to be bigger you still need something you can access and make changes from anywhere even if you have an office assistant.

Going back to email marketing: Over the last 3-4 years we have been able to maintain a solid email marketing automation process that rocks! We touch base with clients depending on what segment they are in within our email process. We tag them based on where in the buyer's journey they are and follow up with leads accordingly. We also follow up with current clients and ex-clients, all with the goal of increasing our client list and growing our company.

Our CRM which is short for Customer Relationship Management software (application or platform), is where you could keep names, emails, customer history, dispatch emails based on what type of clients they may be, or set alerts to follow up with clients depending on the client's needs. This is also the software where you set your emails and put campaigns together to dispatch emails automatically so everything becomes automatic.

The excel screenshot below gives you some ideas on how to use email marketing combined with other digital marketing platforms. By providing links to some of these other platforms you help your customers think of you as an expert in your area.

MARKETING PLAN - NEW CUSTOMERS (2015)

B2B	Jan	Feb	March	April	May	June	July	August	Sept	October	November	December	TOTAL ANTICIPATED PROSPECTS
													0
Monthly Blog Post	15	15	15	15	15	15	15	15	15	15	15	15	180
Ongoing Referral Marketing Campaign	5	5	5	5	5	5	5	5	5	5	5	5	60
Webinar on Special Moving Circumstances	20				20				20				60
YouTube Video			15	15	15	15	15	15	15	15	15		135
LinkedIn	2	2	2	2	2	2	2	2	2	2	2		22
Property Management Conference				20	20								40
Local Networking Events	10		10				10		10		10	10	60
											TOTAL B2B		557
B2C													
Facebook	20	20	20	20	20	20	20	20	20	20	20	20	200
Facebook Ad	40	40	40	40	40	40	40	40	40	40	40	40	400
YouTube Bloopers Video (What happens when you move yourself)					40	40	40	40	40	40	40	40	280
Refer a Friend Campaign		35	35	35	35	35	35	35	35	35	35	35	350
Google Adwords Campaigns	60	60	60	60	60	60	60	60	60	60	60	60	600
College Grad Facebook Campaign							75	75	75	75			300
											TOTAL B2C		2130

2015 Prospects Needed	
B2B	461
B2C	2,000

Figure 6 Sales & Marketing Pipeline Sample

This lesson coming up is important to ensure you can sleep at night. I love to sleep so I never cut corners, we pay all the necessary taxes, pay our staff as employees instead of contractors, we pay the necessary insurance to cover major issues that may arise with clients and employees, and pay according to our state's requirements. In MA according to our attorneys we must pay travel time so we also pay travel time between jobs unlike many other companies in the area...we just really like to sleep and have a clear mind with no malicious intent of any kind so we treat our employees right, we treat our customers with the respect they deserve and in return we are able to continue to grow and create an amazing team.

CHAPTER 7 - ADVICE ON KEY OPERATIONAL PROCEDURES

The lack of basic operational procedures, caused us a lot of trouble the first year or so. We had some procedures, but not enough of them, so everything was in my head instead of being in paper which was a major mistake. We sort of went along with how things were done until we got it right – it wasn't until the second year of operations that we started writing an operational plan. DON'T DO THIS.

You should have an operational plan (OP) from day one and update it as you go. From how the office will take the calls and respond to emails to how the employees will be dispatched in the morning, everything should be covered in the plan.

Make sure to develop a 'telephone script form' so you and your staff always ask the same questions to each client. The phone script would help to train new office staff. I highly recommend putting together an office manager training manuals, maid training managers, floor maintenance manuals, and a phone script just for commercial customers.

And just as important as it is to get your first customers and have procedures in place, hiring becomes a key component of how successful your company will be. Your employees can make you or break you literary in this case. Service companies relay on labor to provide 'the service / for product companies the product is it for service companies employees are the key to an excellent customer experience. And it is for this reason that hiring is significant in how much money you can make with your cleaning service. Although you should hire and have enough staff on hand, you have to do it strategically and do it well to avoid high turnover and all the nightmares that comes with replacing your cleaners often.

Don't hire anyone just because you need someone. It's so obvious and I thought I was following this rule from day 1 but the reality of it is that the 1st year although we did turn some applicants away because they were so obvious they were not good for us. We did too hire out of necessity. There were times when we were turning an employee every 2 month in the first year and it was very tough for us to hire, train, fire or have someone resigned on us, it was tough and it was a problem we were able to deal with because we were very small. The 1st year we did $125k in sales so we were so small that dealing with turnover issues was difficult but manageable for us. But eventually we realized that if we were going to grow 3 or 4 times within 2 years we needed to do better hiring and better training and better on-going quality inspections. We started interviewing the applicants with 2 managers or 2 different interviews. That way if we had 2 managers / owners decide if yes or no. it made a huge difference. Turnover in our industry is the #1 challenge we have nationwide and perhaps globally. Each time you have turnover, you have to spend time advertising the job, interviewing, training and integrating that team member to the team, you could also have customer complaints b/c of poor quality, customer turnover because they are not happy with so many different faces visiting their so often. Turnover is really a business-sucking problem. Decrease employee turnover and you will increase your net profits.

I know the graph below is very hard to read but I wanted to give you an idea of how to organize yourself to from pre-hiring to your 3 months, 6 months and yearly performance reviews. Basically you will have each employee name, the interview date, employee document signatures forms, review of company policies, meeting with trainer, everything gets spelled out for each major action task needed to hire and keep an employee performing at your company's standards.

Options for the gray columns:	Not Yet Started / In Progress / Complete	Finalize Background Check			Employee Documents - Signatures			Review Company Policies			1:1 Meeting with Training Manager			Formally Introduce New Hire to Team			Watch Training Videos			Cleaning Job Shadow Day 1			Cleaning Job Shadow Day 2			First Check In			30-Day Check In	
Employee Num	Employee Name (Last, First)	Hire Date	Finalize Back	Goal	Date Complete	Note	Empl Docu	Goal	Date Complete	Note	Revi Com	Goal	Date Complete	Note	1:1 Mee	Goal	Date Comp	Note	Form ally Intro	Goal	Date Comp	Note	Watc h	Goal	Date Comp	Note	Clean ing Job	Goal	Date Comp	Note	Clean ing Job	Goal	Date Comp	Note	First Check In	Goal	Date Comp	Note	30-Day Check In	Goal	Date Comp	Note
1	XXXX, XXXX	5/17/11	Complete / Not Yet Started / In Progress				Started				Started				Started				Started				Started				Started				Started				Started				Started			

Figure 8 Employee Retention & Recruitment Tool Sample

CHAPTER 8 – GET YOUR SWOT ANALYSIS DONE!

The Strengths, Weaknesses, Opportunities, and Threats' analysis is actually very important for you to do prior to deciding what type of services you offer and what strategies you use. It can also help you establish short and long-term goals. Basically, the name says it all: S is for Strength, W is for Weakness, O is for Opportunity and T is for Threats. The magic happens when you sit down and really give some thought to why you are going to exist in the marketplace. What makes you unique? It could be the smallest thing that gives you an edge, just make sure it's true, something that you can do and that adds value to your service, something customers would appreciate. Nowadays a lot of business owners instead of doing a full in-depth SWOT analysis they are using a competitive analysis and then listing the SWOT analysis to figure out easier how they can compete in the marketplace. The competitive analysis gives you opportunity to see which holes your competitors have in the local market and by recognizing them especially if your competitors are not good at marketing then you can become really good at marketing in order to compete better even if you are not anything that's quite different than your competition. I have seen this and have done it myself where we have become a really good local brand so even though we are not doing anything different than our #1 competitor we are still pretty high in the customer mind so they would hire us versus our #1 competitor simply because we did a good job at branding / marketing / reaching the customer in a way that appears much more professional.

The competitive analysis is going to help you figure out the competition in the market. Who are the players, how long they have been around, what are they are known for, what they need to do better, do they have a strong online presence on social media, blogs, media? Do they do adwords campaigns, what page do they rank on Google, how do they rank on Yelp, how many stars and what are the complaints? Are they responding to reviews? Can you do better than they are in these areas and how? This could be useful especially for your sales and marketing plan.

You can find some of this information online, but some may require you to head to your library and use the business session of your local library to access financial data. For example, in Boston we have the Kirsten Library. I also pay $3500 per year to have access to Hoovers database with access to 3600 contact emails and 15,000 downloads. If I have to do it again I would grow my list organically from day 1 of business. Ask your clients to subscribe to your email, network and let people add them to your newsletter/emails unless they indicate otherwise, set up easy ways for people to join your mailing list and as the weeks go by you will see your list start to grow. Note: Any database out there won't be 100% perfect. I was very upset when I started getting leads with bad email addresses but eventually I calculated the ROI for the $3500 Hoovers database and I did enough business from this database alone, of course before we had a positive return on the $3500. The first 6 months we saw little positive outcomes. I was starting to panic because I had spent money on the database and hiring a virtual assistant to download and clean that data so it was about over $6000 spent on email marketing alone. I was getting nervous because we were being asked for price, met with client but I knew my closing rate was only 30% so I knew that to acquire a new client 3 had to see 10 clients and I was not attracting enough people to request a quote until then slowly and very slowly at first some large companies started to engage with the emails we sent. Initially they would say something like, how much do you charge, or this is what I have is that something you would be interested in? after a couple of months we started to get a few even larger companies email us and soon enough we made enough to cover the investment we made in email marketing. Within the following year we had attracted enough clients and we knew that we were now into something really good, really great actually.

Before you go off to get a database or list from a list broker, you will need to develop your sales & marketing strategic plan so hold your horses before spending so much money! We'll go over the sales & Marketing strategic plan in this guide.

These analyses will help you figure out where you can have a good chunk of the market and be successful, where you are already successful, and what other opportunities you may want to go after in order to stay competitive.

For me, a national, though indirect, competitor was, Homejoy a company similar to Handy.com where clients logged in, booked a cleaning online, and paid merely $20 per hour and sometimes $20 per cleaning! Who can survive on those rates? Well, Homejoy got so much venture capital that their strategy was to come strong in all the major cities and dominate the market. They closed their doors after being hit with multiple labor lawsuits. Consumers were calling and asking how come we couldn't charge the same or similar rates to Homejoy and we had to explain how and why we were different! Leads will get quotes from us and, go to homejoy.com and handy.com to check the difference, then email us to see if we could be around the same rate. When we said no, they booked with Homejoy or handy.com. It was very disappointing; customers wanted the 5-star hotel clean experience but they wanted to pay $20 per hour instead of the $40 per hour we charge per maid. The key lesson here is to know that you cannot compete and win all the clients in your city. It's better to be selective on who you want as a client and only worry about them but at the same time keep an eye open for what's happening in the industry to make sure its not affecting you directly.

Going back to the SWOT Analysis and Competitive Analysis - Think also about your Inspirational Competitor. Who is the ultimate company you wish you could be like 3-5 years from now? What do they do, how do they do it, why are they special, how do they communicate with their clients, what type of advertising do they do, how are their employees trained, etc. If your inspirational competitor is in your market, then you must schedule a cleaning with them and take notes on every step. How they talk to you on the phone, what emails did you receive, did you get a confirmation call or text, how was the service overall, did the maids act or behave in a specific way, how was the cleaning, did they follow up with you after the cleaning and how, would you schedule a 2nd cleaning with them, etc. What is attracting you to them? Think hard and write everything down. Do the same for 2 more companies. Perhaps even schedule the cleaning and cancel and see how they respond. You want to be analytical and figure out what you can do better. Can you provide the same level of service? If that's an easy yes, then you need to find another inspirational company within your industry to challenge yourself and your staff.

One key question that every new cleaning company owners has is "how should I price my services?" In all online forums, offline meetings, business classes I have attended and anywhere else I look, this is the #1 question that business owners have. What I find quite interesting is that the answer is so widely different for all cleaning business owners because it depends on so many things. But what worries me the most is when I see a business owner jump online asking the same question every day or every week, it basically means that they do not have a system for calculating price. There could be nothing more dangerous than a business owner quoting off the top of their heads or based on feelings or just by observing an account without doing hard number calculations.

So let's review in great detail how I calculate price to give you a really solid idea. Also check myhousecleaningbiz.com and myjanitorialstore.com both sites have great spreadsheets and formulas to help you understand how to calculate price. They also have webminars and audio seminars on the subject. I highly recommend you check out these sites and resources it's well worth the money to do so.

CHAPTER 9 – HOW TO CALCULATE THE PRICE
(MORE ON THIS LATER AS WELL)...

If you join Myhousecleaningbiz.com or thejanitorialstore.com or any of the other sites listed as resources, they will have forms and information on how to calculate price very methodologically. I highly recommend doing so if you are starting your business. The method below is what I use for my company, but there are companies that charge by square footage instead of the hour so you have to figure out what works best for you.

Here is a formula I use to figure out prices in my Boston Market:

- What's the Hourly Rate (Wages) we need to pay our employee to keep them long-term and provide quality service? Let's say its $11-$14 per hour for basic cleaning services.

- How much in taxes, insurance, workers compensation, benefits, and bonuses on average per employee ---this may be 15% to 20% on top of their hourly rate. So, if an employee makes $15 per hour, multiply that by 17% = $2.55. Add $15/hour + $2.55 and the real hourly wage for an employee that makes $15 per hour is $17.55 per hour with taxes, benefits, workers comp, etc. This does not include overtime.

- For each account we manage, there is a 'management overhead' associated with the account especially because we schedule random inspections for each account to ensure the cleaners are doing their jobs. Let's say this is 1-3% of total revenues per account. For us the average is 2.5-3%. It can certainly be higher if the client requires daily or weekly facilities inspections. Part of the management fee also includes handling purchasing for the supplies needed to service the client. And there is also the fact that an office staff member has to handle payroll and pay your cleaners on a weekly basis. Don't forget there is training associated for each employee you hire as well. On average, it takes at least 2 weeks and most likely longer before the new cleaner is able to clean an area without a team leader behind them to check the work.

- Once you have all of your costs broken down and you know your true hourly rate, don't forget you also have to consider the profit you want and include that as your hourly rate.
- Our hourly rate is $44 per hour per cleaner. In the Boston Market this is a competitive rate. For you it may be less or more.

After we did the 2 coupon deals never again did we discount our services until late in 2016 when I started experimenting with small discounts and promotional offers! In my opinion, the moment you start discounting your services you are telling your clients – this is the real amount I could be charging so you are really being overcharged. And because we are selling a 5-star clean experience, we don't believe in discounting *too* much. We charge what we need to charge, the same amount whether we are fully booked or not. It keeps our brand strong. Obviously discounting works for retailers, hotels, and even cleaning services, but I don't want to take the chance that I may diminished my brand, the one that took me so long to build. Thus, we provided special offers to non-profit organizations and our current on-call client list but discounting is not something we do all the time.

As you start acquiring and learning the business one thing you should do is to always track your metrics.

How to Hit $1,000,000 In your Cleaning Company

Avg Cleaning Rate	$210			100	
Goal is $1,000,000	$1,000,000			1000000	
How many week-days in a year	260	(does not include working on weekends)		260	
Avg Cleaning Rate	210			100	
̷ many cleanings in weekdays/year?	4762	18.3150183	cleanings per day	10000	so 10,000 cleanings per year
				38.4615385	so 39 cleanings per day if your avg cleaning rate is $100
How Many Cleanings in a Month	396.8253968				
How Many Cleanings in a Week	91.575796				
How Many Cleanings in a day?	18.3151592	So you need to do 18-19 cleanings per day			
How many teams of 3	3.7	5 houses per team per day		6.41025641	you'll need 6 to 7 teams of 3 maids to get to $1,000,000
How many teams of 2	6	3 houses per team per day		9.61538462	you'll need 9 to 10 teams of 2 maids to get to $1,000,000

Plus extra 1-2 employees to cover sick days, etc. Plus 2 office staff to handle customer service, employee phone calls, perhaps 2 supervisors and bookkeeper

Figure 9 Sample of Cleaning Visits Needed to Achieve Your Goals Calculation

Which Metrics you should Analyze to Track Progress in your Business?

Metrics are a way for you to check-in with yourself and your business on a daily, weekly, monthly, quarterly, or yearly basis. This is the way we know if we are on track or if we need to adjust our plan.

Business Metrics Suggestions:

- Total New Customers Gained Per Month – have a clear goal and match the actual compared to 'forecast' numbers so you can determine how you are doing every month based on this metric.
- Revenue per Quarter – again you should have a forecasted amount and track the actual numbers so you can determine how successful you are being at meeting your forecast for the week, month, quarter and year. This is a key measure.
- Direct Field Labor Percentage – Total Labor Expense divided by total revenues – this does not include management salaries – should be less than 48%.
- Profit Margin per Job: Revenues Per Job minus Payroll & Supplies divided by Revenues per Job – this will give us a good target to know which jobs are "Good" and which Jobs are "Fair" Or "Poor".

- Gross Client Margin per Job – ((Revenues – (Labor per Job + Supplies) / Revenues) – this is another key metric because you may be charging enough but your labor is so high that you may not be breaking even. If that's the case, you need to evaluate your operations and pay structure.

- Profit Margin – Goal 20%.

- Customer Loss Rate (Measure by taking Lost Client per Quarter Divided by Beginning Clients in that Quarter = Customer Loss Rate %) – should be 2% or less per year -

- Employee Turnover / Employee Retention – this basically helps you figure out if there is a company culture problem if you have too much employee leaving the company.

Want more about metrics? Head over to tremendouslife.com and see what else we have available for you.

Your Cleaning Company Name Here

SAMPLE ONLY

	HISTORICAL		FINANCIAL GOALS					KEY:
	2012	% of Revenue	2013	2014	2015	2016		Feed
Sales:								Calculation
Cleaning Services	$ 689,136.51	87.41%	$ 758,050.16	$ 1,174,977.75	$ 1,321,849.97	$ 1,454,034.97	<-copy formula	Input
Floor Services	$ 77,780.28	9.87%	$ 127,559.66	$ 178,583.52	$ 200,906.46	$ 231,042.43	<-copy formula	
Other	$ 21,468.88	2.72%	$ 24,791.54	$ 37,891.26	$ 42,627.67	$ 47,171.64	<-copy formula	
Total Sales	**$ 788,385.67**	**100.00%**	**$ 910,401.36**	**$ 1,391,452.53**	**$ 1,565,384.10**	**$ 1,732,249.04**	<-copy formula	
Cost of Goods Sold:								
Automobile	$ 25,129.87	3.19%	$ 29,019.13	$ 44,352.69	$ 49,896.77	$ 55,215.61	<-copy formula	
Credit card fees	$ 13,396.50	1.70%	$ 15,469.83	$ 23,644.00	$ 26,599.50	$ 29,434.93	<-copy formula	
Field staff payroll	$ 334,244.02	42.40%	$ 661,500.00	$ 784,000.00	$ 906,500.00	$ 1,029,000.00	<-copy formula	
Janitorial supplies	$ 16,195.22	2.05%	$ 18,701.70	$ 28,583.57	$ 32,156.52	$ 35,584.30	<-copy formula	
Other*	$ 19,337.83	2.45%	$ 22,330.68	$ 34,130.09	$ 38,396.35	$ 42,489.28	<-copy formula	
Property admin	$ 16,167.95	2.05%	$ 18,670.21	$ 28,535.44	$ 32,102.37	$ 35,524.38	<-copy formula	
Workers' comp	$ 9,167.78	1.16%	$ 10,762.18	$ 12,755.17	$ 14,748.17	$ 16,741.16	<-copy formula	
Total COGS	**$ 433,639.17**	**55.00%**	**$ 776,453.72**	**$ 956,000.97**	**$ 1,100,399.69**	**$ 1,243,989.66**	<-copy formula	
Expenses:								
Automobile - office	$ 27,767.50	3.52%	$ 81.00	$ 81.00	$ 81.00	$ 81.00	<-copy formula	
Health insurance - owners	$ 5,727.22	0.73%	$ 5,727.22	$ 5,727.22	$ 5,727.22	$ 5,727.22	<-copy formula	
Human resources	$ 5,753.72	0.73%	$ 6,754.37	$ 8,005.18	$ 9,255.98	$ 10,506.79	<-copy formula	
Insurance	$ 9,276.94	1.18%	$ 10,712.70	$ 16,373.23	$ 18,419.89	$ 20,383.39	<-copy formula	
Marketing	$ 54,079.08	6.86%	$ 54,079.08	$ 54,079.08	$ 54,079.08	$ 54,079.08	<-copy formula	
Other**	$ 28,879.97	3.66%	$ 29,168.77	$ 29,460.46	$ 29,755.06	$ 30,052.61	<-copy formula	
Payroll	$ 115,845.29	14.69%	$ 135,845.29	$ 135,845.29	$ 135,845.29	$ 135,845.29	<-copy formula	
Professional fees	$ 9,695.74	1.23%	$ 9,695.74	$ 9,695.74	$ 9,695.74	$ 9,695.74	<-copy formula	
Rent	$ 13,093.52	1.66%	$ 13,093.52	$ 13,093.52	$ 13,093.52	$ 13,093.52	<-copy formula	
Training & development	$ 7,026.52	0.89%	$ 8,248.52	$ 9,776.03	$ 11,303.53	$ 12,831.04	<-copy formula	
Travel	$ 5,201.84	0.66%	$ 6,006.91	$ 9,180.93	$ 10,328.55	$ 11,429.54	<-copy formula	
Total Expenses	**$ 282,347.34**	**35.81%**	**$ 279,413.12**	**$ 291,317.67**	**$ 297,584.86**	**$ 303,725.22**	<-copy formula	

▷   Forecast   2012 P&L   +

Figure 10 Forecasting Tool

Health insurance - owners	$	...	...		$	...	$	...	$	...	$	...	<-copy formula

Human resources	$ 5,753.72	0.73%		$ 6,754.37	$ 8,005.18	$ 9,255.98	$ 10,506.79	<-copy formula
Insurance	$ 9,276.94	1.18%		$ 10,712.70	$ 16,373.23	$ 18,419.89	$ 20,383.39	<-copy formula
Marketing	$ 54,079.08	6.86%		$ 54,079.08	$ 54,079.08	$ 54,079.08	$ 54,079.08	<-copy formula
Other**	$ 28,879.97	3.66%		$ 29,168.77	$ 29,460.46	$ 29,755.06	$ 30,052.61	<-copy formula
Payroll	$ 115,845.29	14.69%		$ 135,845.29	$ 135,845.29	$ 135,845.29	$ 135,845.29	<-copy formula
Professional fees	$ 9,695.74	1.23%		$ 9,695.74	$ 9,695.74	$ 9,695.74	$ 9,695.74	<-copy formula
Rent	$ 13,093.52	1.66%		$ 13,093.52	$ 13,093.52	$ 13,093.52	$ 13,093.52	<-copy formula
Training & development	$ 7,026.52	0.89%		$ 8,248.52	$ 9,776.03	$ 11,303.53	$ 12,831.04	<-copy formula
Travel	$ 5,201.84	0.66%		$ 6,006.91	$ 9,180.93	$ 10,328.55	$ 11,429.54	<-copy formula
Total Expenses	**$ 282,347.34**	**35.81%**		**$ 279,413.12**	**$ 291,317.67**	**$ 297,584.86**	**$ 303,725.22**	<-copy formula

Net Other Income:

Net other income	$ 3,983.92	0.51%		$ 4,600.50	$ 7,031.38	$ 7,910.30	$ 8,753.51	<-copy formula

Net Income	$ 76,383.08	9.69%		$ (140,864.98)	$ 151,165.27	$ 175,309.85	$ 193,287.67	<-copy formula

				-15%	11%	11%	11%	
Key Assumptions:				2013	2014	2015	2016	
Residential growth rate				10.0%	55.0%	12.5%	10%	<-enter proj. growth percent
Commercial growth rate				64.0%	40.0%	12.5%	15%	<-enter proj. growth percent
Field staff employees	$ 23.00			27	32	37	42	<-enter proj. employees
Current field staff payroll / employee	$ 24,000.00							
Bonuses / employee	$ 500.00	<-enter avg. bonus / employee						
Workers comp / employee	$ 398.60							
Number of leased cars	$ -			9	9	9	9	<-enter proj. cars required
Automobile - office / car	$ 9.00							
IR / employee	$ 250.16							
New hire salary	$ 20,000.00	<-enter sales position salary						
Training / employee	$ 305.50							
Other** growth rate	1%							

Other includes breakage, COGS, equipment rental COGS, extra service expense, key return, laundry, subcontractor and supplies / labor fully invoiced

* Other includes bank service charges, business licenses / permits, charitable contributions, dues & subscriptions, employee dining, equipment repair expenses, exec meeting dining, interest expense, laundry, mar

Figure 11 Forecasting Tool Net Profits View and additional input

CHAPTER 10 - MY ABSOLUTE BEST MARKETING TIPS I COULD GIVE RIGHT NOW!

Exercise Sample: Determine what are your service goals for this coming year thru next 5 years. For example: you can have service goals for different target markets such: Company X will provide residential cleaning to college master / PhD students & graduates in the Boston / Cambridge Area to apartment tenants who are within 3-miles radius from Harvard University. We will service 10 recent graduates per day which is 50 per week and potentially 216.5 (50 clients per 4.33 weeks per month)

What are the pros and cons of your customer base?

What are the current pain points they have in common? Perhaps a big problem is that they want a clean home because they are starting a new job and or very busy finishing their studies that they have no time to clean but they are also on a tight budget so what could you do to make your company appealing? Perhaps offering buy 10 light cleanings and 1 deep cleaning to be scheduled every 3 months?

You have to figure out how big the market is: you could find this easily by looking up the stats on google or the big universities near Harvard such as MIT – how many masters and PhD students they have each year in their campus (not online students)?
How many can you service and perform so well that they will want to refer you to their friends?

How would they find you? Online, flyers at the university? Yelp? Print media? How much would it cost you? How soon do you expect to acquire your first few clients? Why would the customer buy from you?

What are the worst-case scenario, okay and best scenarios for how many clients you would need to make this a good return on your time and efforts?

You have to develop the benefits of why the customer would buy from you: give them lots of benefits not features. Can they text message you instead of having to call you on an office? A lot of our customers prefer to text the office staff so we have a number just for texting that is monitored constantly from 7:30am to 5pm Mon to Fridays.

Here is an example of how to break down the numbers on how many customers you would need to convert from leads to customers if they find you on your site. Here you can see that you really need to start with as many people as possible before you can convert someone from just someone that may show some interest in your company to someone that is actually willing to pay you for your service.

Let's say you have about 3000 potential customers available within the 3-miles radius that may be able to afford your services. Out of 3000 for the entire year, you know that perhaps 10% could become your clients but you also know they all won't become clients at the same time so how would you get your first client, the 2nd client and so on? If 100 of these potential clients are searching online every month for a cleaning service, how can you get them to call you and out of those that show some interest, how would you continue to move them towards understanding that they need your company.

Advertising –What Works and Potential New Channels – Marketing Plan by end of year 20xx

must be updated to reflect updated channels based on ROI from the current channels used.

	Currently Use	Plan to Use or Continue to Use	Annual Expense	Comments
Brochures	Yes/No	Yes/No	xxxxxx	Brochure for Mailing & To Provide during On-Site Visitations
Postcards for Trade Shows & Leave Behinds	Yes/No	Yes/No	xxxxxx	
Yelp	Yes/No	Yes/No	xxxxxx	
Media Advertising, Public Relations	Yes/No	Yes/No	xxxxxx	
Print (Newspaper, Magazine)	Yes/No	Yes/No	xxxxxx	Who will develop the ad copy?
Online	Yes/No	Yes/No	xxxxxx	In-House & Freelance
Social Media	Yes/No	Yes/No		In-House
Blogs	Yes/No	Yes/No	xxxxxx	
YouTube / Video Marketing	Yes/No	Yes/No	xxxxxx	In-House
Advertising Specialties	Yes/No	Yes/No	xxxxxx	

for Trade Shows				
Direct Mail or Email Campaign	Yes/No	Yes/No	xxxxxx	
Website & monthly maintenance	Yes/No	Yes/No	xxxxxx	
Trade Shows Table Registration and Staff	Yes/No	Yes/No	xxxxxx	The first 2 shows we learned and the last 4 years we rocked!
Exhibits/signs	Yes/No	Yes/No	xxxxxx	
Informal Marketing/Networking	Yes/No	Yes/No	xxxxxx	
Memberships/ Regional Meetings & Conventions for Educational Purposes	Yes/No	Yes/No	xxxxxx	
Entertainment	Yes/No	Yes/No	xxxxxx	
Professional Assistance (Legal, Designers)	Yes/No	Yes/No	xxxxxx	
Mobile Web Design	Yes/No	Yes/No	xxxxxx	
Sales Staff:			xxxxxx	
Salary				
Commission/bonus		8-10%?	xxxxxx	

Expenses		Cell / Gas Reimbursement / etc	xxxxxx	
Retargeting	?	?	?	?
PPC	?	?	?	?
Wrap all Vehicles	?	?	?	?
Social Media				
Total				

Other Marketing Tips To Make 6 Figures Starting Today: This won't work unless you apply these tips consistently – do it every single week, every single month and you'll see huge success and increased revenues.

#1 You need a mobile friendly site. In today's economic more than 50% of your potential clients will try to find you while they are using their cellular or ipads. Therefore, Google even gives better ranking to sites that are mobile friendly / mobile reactive, meaning that your site changes based on what type of device is being used. Don't get too confused, your website developer should be able to do this for cheap. In some cases a basic plugin is all it takes.

#2 Develop an email campaign for at least 3 different scenarios read the ebook on How to Triple Your Revenues with Marketing Automation for Your Cleaning Company or buy Predictable Revenue book –an excellent book I highly recommend it. Let's start with scenario #1 which is a potential customer so the email campaigns have to help them choose you as their cleaning service. Scenario 2 is for current clients so you can cross sell to them and upsell them. Scenario 3 is to ask for referrals. Both your potential and current clients should get these emails. Each email campaign could consist of 5 to 6 emails to be automatic dispatched every 2 weeks or so. And make sure you put together e-newsletter to dispatch to potential and current clients so at least once a month they hear from you.

#3 On your site develop a couple of infographics for your potential new clients and have them give you their name and email in exchange for the infographic. This helps you appear as an authority in the industry and the customers will trust you more. The infographic should be about a topic that your potential clients are googling on Google or a video you put together for those clients that are doing a search on Youtube. For example: How to find the best cleaning company in your city and state. Then you will give them methods to find and research the local companies and ideas on how to interview the companies and do a spreadsheet or pros and cons list of who they will hire etc. It does not need to be complicated at all.

#4 Find a Voice Messaging platform such Slybroadcast to send voice messages to your clients to provide special discounts and induce sales. The voice messages sound personal and clients will think you called them, couldn't reach them so you left them a message saying "Hi there, this is xxxx at tel #, I wanted to reach out because this month we are running a special promotion to previous one time clients only and I wanted to make sure you knew so you could take advantage of it, if you book this week, we'll give you $50 off cleaning for the month of January. Please call us at xxxxxxx, thanks so much, your name and company name and make sure to repeat the tel #. You want to give the telephone number at the beginning and end so if they have to listen again to your message the tel number is right at the beginning – it makes a big difference in how many people will stop from calling just because you make them listen to the whole message to listen again to the tel #.

We used this several times and it works extremely well. I highly recommend you to implement this idea immediately. If I had done this from the first year we would have been doubling the business much faster because when we started, even the people that said you know for some reason your message was breaking up so I couldn't hear all of it, they called the office and we then explain, this is why we called, would you be interested in booking the service –and the answer more than 60% of the time was yes!

#5 Keep good records of your promotions. Make sure you are not discounting all the time. For example, you could have a discount in January but in February you could simply do a mass voice message even if it's to 10 people and say – I am just calling to follow up and make sure we are providing you with an awesome service. As you know, we provide fridge cleaning, oven service, carpet cleaning, etc. – if we can help you with any additional service please let us know. And make sure you follow the tip above in #4 about the tel phone etc. – you want to cross and upsell your customers whenever possible without sounding too salesclerk. In this case, the main objective was to call and follow up to ensure your customer is happy so the fact that you say and as you know we also provide x, y and z makes you sound like you are adding more value to the customer instead of just simply selling them on things they don't need.

CHAPTER 11 - MAKING CHANGES AND SETTING GOALS

After completing an operational audit, we encountered a few areas of opportunity for improvement in order to grow. This challenge also served to help us increase customer satisfaction tremendously. We identified three major processes that are scheduled for immediate improvement included below.

Let me just say that the operational audit was simply a meeting of our staff going over the specific steps on what happens from when a client decides to do business with us to how we follow to ensure they are happy with our service so nothing overly complicated.

This is how I broke down the tasks to identify clear ways for us to always follow the same process and ensure we increase customer satisfaction.

#1 Customer Satisfaction / Communication –this is a major aspect of our operations that we want to improve.

Step #1: Office assistant to text clients as follows:

- Text via Google Voice
    - Text New Clients after Initial Cleaning to Get Feedback
    - Text Reg clients weekly & biweekly clients text every 2 months to get feedback – put an alarm on scheduling platform to get reminders to dispatch texts.
    - Text Reg monthly clients every 3 months to get feedback
    - Text clients who complete an online quote request – We will first email and call them but if the clients do not answer within 2 hours, we will also text them.
- Email Tasks are to be as follows:
    - Email clients who have completed their first cleanings and did not book regular service. If your target market prefers a call, make sure you pick up the phone and call the client to ask for feedback and also to ask them to book regular service. A good amount of our older (seniors) clients prefer phone calls instead of texting or emails.
    - Email inspection reports to commercial clients and regular residential clients based on client's preferences

#2 Training Program

- **Attracting & Hiring 'the right' candidates**
    - Better Application (In English and Spanish)
    - Interviewing Process
        - Set of interviews
            - Application must be completely answered
            - Application must be done in-house (this will prevent to give out so many applications and to ensure that applicant is the person answering the questions
        - Scout Talent Test
            - This test helps us determine if the person has the qualities we desire in people
    - Hiring Process
        - Background test completed

- Reference check
- Get paperwork ready for employee's signature

- **Training**
  - Orientation
    - Schedule first day of orientation to meet all staff members & watch first set of videos
    - 2nd Day question the learning from day 1 and show floor care & bathroom care training videos
  - Team Training
    - 3rd Day one-on-one training at our training units
  - Individual Training Sessions
    - Training with Lead Trainers
  - On the job training
    - One test day by 2nd week –Employee will clean by them without supervision. Once done the Training Manager will solicit his/her input.
    - Schedule 2nd day for employee to clean alone again and for Training Manager to give input after completion.
    - Once Trainee knows how to clean a house, the trainee then learns to clean a common space area in buildings such as hallways, elevator tracks, elevator panels, floors, etc.
    - Training will depend on the position hired for but all employees must learn to clean a house since it requires more attention to details

- **Seminars**
  - Specific Workshops for all Team Members
    - Follow up Training to refresh Team Member's knowledge
    - Training on Customer Service
    - Training on Corporate Athlete

  - Training Programs for Owners, Managers, Supervisors & Office Staff
    - Customer Service Programs
    - Employment Law / HR Topics
    - Corporate Athlete Program
    - Landmark Forum Program
    - Ongoing Programs to follow up on both Corporate Athlete & Landmark Forum

#3 Quality Assurance

- First Cleaning and office assistant calls/ texts to get customer feedback

- Regular Service Follow up
- Work Orders – Adding Value thru:
  - Auto Inspections Emailed to Clients
  - Allow clients to place work orders in the system
  - Place work orders in the system and email to client for their verifications
    - Meet with clients on a quarterly basis to gather feedback

Here is another example of a process we wanted to improve: We used to let the client find us, book the service and follow up with us. We needed to change this process immediately to ensure we make it easier for clients to book with us, give us input, and sign up for regular service.

One of the major changes we wanted to implement immediately is a culture of being proactive so we decided that all one-time cleaning clients will receive a text message via Google voice to ask for quick feedback. If the client is happy, we will offer a date and time for a second cleaning. If the client is not happy, we call immediately to find out what went wrong and if we can dispatch a team to return and clean the areas in questions. Immediately after, we will follow up with the client again to ensure 100% happiness.

So the first steps I took was to decide in paper how this would look and what would be required from my team to make it happen.

- Step #1 Create a template for each text message so the office staff has a few options for sending the text messages based if it's a new client, existing client, message if client is happy or upset, etc. Text messages must be fun but professional.

- Step #2 Office assistant must call everyone that sends an email for both residential and commercial clients. Currently we simply respond back with an email. Starting immediately, we will reply with an email and call within 1 hour if we do not get a response back.

- Step #3 Set up an auto remainder to do 30, 60, 90 and every 6-months performance feedback with each team member. Automating the schedule through our scheduling manager program and Google calendar would help us ensure that performance reviews are always consistent. This will help us determining which employees need further training in specific areas to ensure the best customer service possible. The performance review considered the customer feedback we received on a daily basis. We tracked that in a spreadsheet and then it would be used during the employee performance feedback.

- For client's quarterly meetings – we will send email invites to secure on site visitations via Google Calendar. We will offer meeting online via Webex to clients that prefer meeting online instead of in person. This will appear to the younger managers and also help to reduce travel time and travel expense (gas, tolls, and parking)

Now you can see all the steps you have to break down before providing instructions to your team or to you on how things have to work. It is important to work out these tasks in paper because by the time you have a solid clear idea, you have to make adjustments. If you have a large team, then you have to have a team meeting to review and make sure you did not miss something important in the new tasks and processes you create. It is important to figure out how are you going to track and ensure that your team is following your orders. If you are doing it yourself you should still have a system in place where you know whether or not you are truly following the processes you put in place for your company.

Conclusion of the first part of this manual:

These are my lessons, mistakes, and secrets to help you earn the financial goals you have for company. Even if you are in business, I hope this ebook can help you grow much faster. If you are new and need more help, feel free to reach out to me directly via email at Victoria_Amador@hotmail.com and stay in touch by visiting my blog at tremendouslife.com. I am in the process of creating a MasterMind Group for cleaning business owners to meet biweekly. I hope you can join us for this MasterMind Group. Join my list at tremendouslife.com

So let's go into what's the info in The 6 Figure Cleaning Business Master Class….this is the action pack part of the manual.

CHAPTER 12 - THE CLEANING BIZ TASK LIST

What are some of the things in your cleaning company that you need to have a clear process for?

- Benefits and competitive matrix / SWOT Analysis
- Metrics to track efficiency thru Payroll
- Rate Template for consistency / Profitable pricing (also known as pricing spreadsheet)
- Bill rate alarms and process
- Closing during holidays rescheduling email template and process
- Dispatching the maids (consider how to pick which teams are assigned to homes for ex based on clients preferences etc)
- Invoice template
- Collection letters (template for 1st notice, 2nd notice, final notice, etc)
- Getting maid's vehicles ready for dispatch?
- AM Dispatch Meeting - what does the manager discuss on a daily basis
- PM Car Drop Off Procedures
- AM Opening/Closing Procedures for maids, office staff, etc.
- AM / PM Overview of Sales, Marketing, Financial, Operational Overviews, etc.
- Video and photo release form for employees
- Hang-up on price – how to go about that?
- Emergency plan during snowstorms? During power out in homes or buildings?
- Background checks
- How to interview / hire / train employees
- Email marketing templates
- Chemicals / purchasing / labels
- Social media – what to post during storms or closed days template
- How to diplomatically respond to online reviews
- How to find employees
- Blog writing
- Employee disciplinary action form

- Current organizational chart (vision organizational chart)
- Sales & Marketing plan (SAMPLE)
- Equipment and product use waiver for clients if they want us to use their equipment / supplies
- Employee's daily record of Tips
- Employee performance review spreadsheet
- Drivers log / team logs
- Smoking / drinking policy form (you should have an employee manual and this must be included in it)
- Tidy up letter for messy clients template
- Referral emails templates
- Quality control worksheet
- Cancellation of services letter – to drop difficult clients
- Production rate tracking
- Quality assurance cleaning guide
- Home inspection form
- Vehicle service maintenance schedule
- Track marketing activities on Google
- Pre-existing surface damage waiver
- Unsecure key waiver form
- Price increase letter template
- Telephone call log tracking template
- Weekly Meeting agenda
- Credit policy for clients
- Email templates for new leads, for on call clients, and for current clients
- Exiting customer survey template
- Theft accusation letter template
- Welcome packet for new clients
- Laundry services and email template
- Window blind cleaning template
- Unable to perform service template
- Received keys – return keys template
- Key log procedures
- Damage/ breakage report email / echosign – procedures

- Complaint follows up email and phone call procedures
- Post construction rates higher than reg deep cleanings – process
- Home walk thru on site forms
- Commercial walk thru on site forms
- Carpet cleaning quote and process template
- Strip and wax quote and process template
- Template of cleaning proposal
- Telephone script for quote requests for residential
- Telephone script for quote requests for commercial
- Telephone script for quote requests for carpet
- Telephone script for quote requests for strip and wax
- Telephone script for quote requests for floor scrubbing
- One copy of the new hire orientation checklist, paperwork (ready for copies) – includes paperwork, schedule time to watch the new hire videos, time to meet with Operations Manager and review all policies, Chemicals, Start Time, etc
- Sample of job description for residential maids (template), for commercial depends if PT or FT
- Disciplinary Warnings – including how to document verbal warnings
- Use of company owned vehicles procedures (in manual?)
- Supervisor performance evaluation
- Request leave of absence form
- Possession of company property form (in manual)
- Nondisclosure and noncompete form (in manual)
- Company turnover report
- Dress code policy (in manual already)
- Vehicle accident report form
- First report of injury form
- Supplies checklist (Purchasing process)
- Invoice sample
- Collection letters -templates
- Customer on-boarding checklist
- Dishonored check template
- Announcing a new service template
- Sales questions to ask new commercial clients

- Sales calls log
- Salesperson agreement form template
- Payroll and GPS tracking form update for payroll
- And more!??

CHAPTER 13 - FINANCIAL OVERVIEW

It's a must to understand where daily sales are at all times. Therefore, a daily login to your financial statements is necessary. Review daily sales either at 7am or after 5pm when invoices for the day has been entered on Quickbooks. Based on the excel Dashboard Template - every day we can track total sales per day and compared to the 'Goal for the Year' to know if we are on track (or not) to achieving daily sales goals.

For example, on 3/28/2016 we were off by just a bit over $1000 in sales. So then, I have to figure out if is it because we didn't have enough deep cleanings, perhaps we changed the invoicing dates for some clients (which have happened and we realized we freaked out for no reason), did we have a snow storm so we scheduled limited people to work? There could be several reasons so a daily dashboard helps us to figure out how are we doing compared to our yearly goal and break it down by month, week and days.

The main areas to pay attention has been summarized in the table below. We track # of deep cleanings, # of floor projects, residential and commercial sales by the day, how many employees for residential and commercial so we can calculate gross margins for both divisions. As you can see the daily gross margin for commercial when compared to residential could be as twice higher!

This daily analysis also helps you to keep track of your marketing investments. Are you getting a good return on investment on Yelp? PR? Flyers etc? Wherever you are putting your marketing dollars, it should be reflected in sales volume. Also if you are putting a lot of money on yelp and you get the clients but then they always complaint, do not like to pay and give you a hard time then maybe you need to figure out if your ads on yelp may be misleading people, or figure out if your team really does have issues or the problem are the yelpers? This analysis could reveal many ways for you to improve your marketing dollars.

Create a spreadsheet to track daily dashboard analysis. If possible, have the office staff fill it in for you at least once per week. Daily would be ideal but it takes times for the office to fill it in so you need to determine if that's the best use for your staff.

One more note: This analysis to be done at least once per month or biweekly could help you also figure out Google Analytics and how your website is doing. The #1 way we get clients is on Google & then on Yelp especially for residential. Google is the #1 form of lead generation for commercial accounts for us. Google analytics can tell us whether our website is working effectively or whether certain pages need to be updated. Perhaps the site headings and subheadings need to be change to better show the benefits of hiring us as cleaning company. We update our website - or do a quick refresh often. Normally we change the banners or headings at least every 2-3 years. It's important to review google analytics and figure out if there are any plugins that need updating, if forms are working, and update it often. Note: It's important to check plugins / forms you have on your website at least once per month if not more often. The worst that can happen is potential clients come to our site and they cannot fill out our forms to requests quotes from us!

Company xyz Daily Dashboard				3/28 Monday
ACTUAL 2012		DIFF	DAILY GOAL FOR 2012	
Residential Sales:	$2,223.00	$458.99	Residential Sales:	$2,681.99	
Total # of Field Employees Res:	15				
Avg Hours Worked Res:	6.92	1400.625			
Gross Margins Res:	37.0%	63.01%			
Daily Revenues for Commercial:	$818.63	$638.90	COM Sales Daily:	$1,457.53	
Total # of Field Employees COM:	3				
Avg Hours Worked COM:	7.5	326.25			
Gross Margins COM:	60.1%	39.85%			
TM Deep Cleaning #:	1		# of Special Projects Needed to Meet Goal		

			for 2012 for total of $45,500		
New XYZ Client #:			1 project per day needed		
Window Cleaning #:					
Floor Scrubbing/ Strip/Waxing #:		1			
Carpet Cleaning #:					
Other (Snow, Painting, etc) #:					
Total # of Special Projects:		1			

The Yelp analysis is especially useful if you are spending money on ads or advertising on yelp. You need to determine whether the money invested is yielding a return on investment. For years, we tracked yelp views, clicks to our site, and then the conversion rate. We ask every client where they found us and make sure we track that to check if our advertising is working or needs improvement. Then we also can track the avg sale per yelp client. Our scheduling software can print out a report so we know the 'source' of each new client per month or regular client per month or however you want to track it, then you take the average and hopefully you'll track that throughout the months and years. This method helps to track month to month fluctuations and which months you could do more push in advertising or email marketing, etc. For example, for us, we know winter is slower so from Nov to March sales are historical lower. With that in mind, we can put together a winter marketing program to increase new "one time' clients or a marketing marketing especially to attract potential clients who would sign up for continuous regular service.

If you want to take it even further, you can compare Yelp vs your other Lead Generation Sources such as Angies List, Home Advisor, Google, Amazon Services, etc. You can then compare which lead generation sites or print media are doing the best and invest your money wisely going forward.

Yelp Analysis from May 2011 to May 31st 2014

Jan Comp	Year '11	Year '12	Year '13	Year '14
User Views		345	452	340
Click to Site		81	138	122
Click Through Rate		23.48%	30.53%	35.88%
Revs	$384.02	$19,528.00	$46,568.00	$51,350.00
FEB Comp	Year '11	Year '12	Year '13	Year '14
User Views		335	388	307
Click to Site		87	100	79
Click Through Rate		25.97%	25.77%	25.73%
Revs	740	$18,815.00	$41,198.00	$54,588.00

March Comp	Year '11	Year '12	Year '13	Year '14
User Views		292	503	298
Click to Site		84	151	78
Click Through Rate		28.77%	30.02%	26.17%
Revs	$7,534.00	$19,827.00	$50,000.	$52,991

Yelp Analysis from May 2011 to May 31st 2014 Sample

Jan Comp	Year '11	Year '12	Year '13	Year '14	Last Yrs Avg	$39,149
User Views		345	452	340	Forecast	$54,461
Click to Site		81	138	122	Actual Revs	$51,350
Click Through Rate		23.48%	30.53%	35.88%	.+ / - Budget?	-$3,111
Revs	$384	$19,528	$46,568	$51,350	Inc from '13 to '14	$4,782
FEB Comp	Year '11	Year '12	Year '13	Year '14	Last Yrs Avg	$38,200
User Views		335	388	307	Forecast	$49,091
Click to Site		87	100	79	Actual Revs	$54,588
Click Through Rate		25.97%	25.77%	25.73%	.+ / - Budget?	$5,497
Revs	$740	$18,815	$41,198	$54,588	Inc from '13 to '14	$13,390

March Comp	Year '11	Year '12	Year '13	Year '14	Last Yrs Avg	$40,939
User Views		292	503	298	Forecast	$57,893
Click to Site		84	151	78	Actual Revs	$52,991
Click Through Rate		28.77%	30.02%	26.17%	.+ / - Budget?	-$4,902
Revs	$7,534	$19,827	$50,000	$52,991	Inc from '13 to '14	$2,991
April Comp	Year '11	Year '12	Year '13	Year '14	Last Yrs Avg	$43,966
User Views		429	453	294	Forecast	$55,061
Click to Site		151	157	78	Actual Revs	$61,352
Click Through Rate		35.20%	34.66%	26.53%	.+ / - Budget?	$6,291
Revs	$2,636	$23,378	$47,168	$61,352	Inc from '13 to '14	$14,184

May Comparison	Year '11	Year '12	Year '13	Year '14	Last Yrs Avg	$52,122
User Views	360	565	599	318	Forecast	$70,139
Clicks to Site	196	178	213	71	Actual Revs	$66,364
Click Through Rate	54.50%	31.50%	35.60%	22.30%	.+ / - Budget?	-$3,775
Revenues	$7,341	$27,755	$62,246	$66,364.00	Inc from '13 to '14	$4,118

Google Analytics

We all know that Google is the #1 for consumers and other businesses to small businesses like us. Besides doing the Search Engine Optimization and perhaps even Google Ad Words etc - you also need to track very closely what's going on with your Google Analytics Page. i've set goals on my Google Analytics page that are check weekly to make sure we are checking on the progress of certain pages within our website.

We have several goals on all websites we manage. For example, we would have a goal to track the visits to specific pages such as:

Goal description

Name: Contact Us -potential submission

SMART_GOAL Goal type:

Destination

Equals to   http://www.tremendousmaid.com/thanks

Why did we wanted to check that? Well, for some odd reason a plugin made our quote request form seem like we were getting hundreds of requests but it was all spam visits with not actual submissions so the goal here is to check how many people actually landed on the thanks page which the only way to get there was to submit a quote request. Then we cross-reference that number with our Customer Relationship Management Software to see how many forms were submitted. There has been time when the numbers don't match especially if somehow spammers get a hold of that page called 'thanks' so we then have to change the page name to make sure we keep spammers away. On another occasion we also had included a link to a specific page on the site and it had a message to increase carpet cleaning services. We tested it for a few months before taking it away and adding a different page. But you could also set a goal on Google Analytics to check how that specific link /page on your site is doing from your invoices or print media or specific lead generation sites.

Google Listing Is Key for Business - GOBY.com/Business

Your business should be listed on google -for us, it's the number one source of finding new clients for both residential and commercial leads. One way to do this is to ensure your business is listed in Google. Simply go to GYBO.com/Business to check how your business shows up on Google. Type in your business name, add your business for free if it isn't on the list and review suggestions on how to improve your presence on Google.

You'll need to verify your business. You'll have to wait for Google to call or send you a postcard in the mail confirming your address with a PIN code that you'll enter it online to verify your account. Basically you'll go online and follow the instructions and insert your PIN where the screen says "Enter Code". Once you confirm your account make sure to follow the tips below to have a great listing on Google.

- ✓ Review the business listing information. Make sure that the telephone number, address, hours of operations, business descriptions are correct. It's vital that you don't overlook this because people searching your business are going to Google first before they find your website. People can call directly from Google and according to Google there are 97% of people looking for businesses via mobile devices so ensuring your website is mobile friendly is huge! (source: Google/ipSos Media CT/Purchased, Understanding Consumer's Local Search Behavior, May 2014)

- ✓ Add photos. Google also confirms that businesses with lots of photos get more views and therefore higher chance of creating a visitor to a paying client.

- ✓ You can also download the Google My Business app for Android in the Google Play Store for IOS in the APP Store. Then you can update your business hours directly from your phone if you need to close early on a specific date, add photos, etc.

- ✓ On the Google listing you can also see "Insights" such as how many customers searched for your business --did they find you direct or did they discovered you by searching for a category, product or service? Did customers find you on Google Maps? Did they visit your site? View Photos or placed a Call? Did they ask for directions to your business? All of this info you can see by the week, month or 90 days...you can download it and keep track of it over the years. It's all very exciting information.

Year to Year Comparison of Google Analytics

Jan Overview	Sessions	User	% New Sessions	Returning Visitors	Pageviews	Pages per Session	Avg Session Time	Bounce Rate
Jan-12	207	173	79%	20.80%	290	1.4	1:32	76.33%
Jan-13	742	525	68%	22%	2162	2.91	2:42	49.33%
Jan-14	416	358	82%	19%	2712	2.47	2:06	43.75%
Jan-15	501	408	76%	24%	1081	2.16	1:50	57.68%
AVG Convertion Rates	366	76%						
New Sessions #	278.3							
Conversion %	13%							
February Overview								
Feb-12	183	150	75.41%	23.50%	264	1.44	1:30	71.04%
Feb-13	579	418	65%	35%	1618	2.79	3:05	52.50%
Feb-14	468	395	80.00%	19.40%	395	1:37	1:37	52%
Feb-15	442	383	0.8281	0.1719	850	1.92	0.0625	0.6697
AVG Convertion Rates	336.5	75.81%						

New Sessions #	255.08 3825							

CHAPTER 14 - PROFITABLE PRICING OVERVIEW

Client Profitability Spreadsheet

15% - 20% profit is typical of residential cleaning companies

15-33% profit is typical for commercial accounts depending on size

The client profitable or client account analysis helps you to figure out how profitable each one of your clients are. It could also help you figure out if your employees are too fast or too slow and hopefully gets you to investigate further what needs to be fixed to provide the client with a great cleaning experience. You should also use it to figure out which clients need a price increase and what that increase should be. When doing the price yearly price increase keep in mind that not all of your clients started service on the same day so you definitely want to do it on a case by case and do it over a certain time frame. Do not increase all clients at the same time or you could lose many clients.

Normally you should strive to do this analysis for all clients every quarter or so to ensure you are keeping a good eye on your employee's productivity. Some things we've found out when doing this is that a client may be asking the cleaner/s for more than what was contracted and thus payroll has increased so a conversation with the client to review the cleaning specs and what was agreed could help fix the issue.

The sample below of the deep cleaning is included because deep cleanings can yield huge revenues for your company. Tracking deep cleanings month over month would help you identify when you need to make changes to meet the customer demands so its imperative to keep track of the deep cleaning metrics.

	Deep Cleaning Analysis: Review of Month to Month Deep Cleanings Comparison Year by Year 2013 to Current									
Year	# of DC January	# of DC February	# of DC March	# of DC April	# of DC May	# of DC June	July	August	September	October
2013 QB	47	33	73	60	71	59	56	60	57	62
Avg Sales per Month QB	$10,063.20	$8,292.45	$15,122.71	$11,613.20	$17,055.90	$15,259.61	$16,438.33	$19,782.54	$18,028.99	$20,411.04
2013 SM	47	33	75	62	69	59	64	59	60	63
2014 QB	28	26	30	36	34	35	52	51	51	26
Avg Sales per Month QB	$10,647.07	$7,429.60	$8,390.83	$11,558.27	$11,304.23	$13,190.21	$17,205.84	$15,303.76	$14,417.04	$7,466.67
2014 scheduling	31	28	29	36	41	36	55	63	72	36

Figure 12 Deep Cleaning Analysis Sample

NOTE:

 If a specific client is below 15% - you need to increase prices. Yes, even if you lose the client.

Commercial Account Analysis Sample

Date Initially Met with Client	Company Name	Monthly Account Value	Time to Close Account
List all one by one			
	Total Monthly Value =	Add all values to get total amount	
	Average per Account =	Take the avg for all accounts -goal is to keep increasing it over time	
Goal $676k by Dec 31, 2014 for commercial sales only			
Monthly Sales Needed	$56,333	*However if we manage to increase the avg account value per month, all these numbers can be completely different.	
#of accounts /year at $800	56.33		
# of accts needed per week	1.076923077	For example: If goal is 676k and we are doing $34,379 per month at the beginning of Jan 1 2017 we need to start producing 21,954 per month to hit that goal. So to get 21,954 in sales per month, we need 27.44 clients valued at $800 per month but obviously you won't get all your clients at the beginning of the year so this just helps you figure out how aggressive your sales team have to be and helps to set your marketing budget.	
we need to see 250 potential leads to get to 75 accounts	57.5		
Proposal per month	20.83333333		
Proposal per week	4.81139338		

*As the years progress you have to also create a Lost Account Analysis to track the accounts you lose for any reason (perhaps the client decided to manage and contract their own in-house employees, hire another company due to lower prices or lack of good quality cleaning, etc).

For our ideal target market -price is not the issue. They are willing to pay what it takes so when a client asks for price do not make it a big deal, say it casually but clearly what's the price structure. Then immediately after providing the price make sure to continue the conversation by saying -'the price is xxx per hour with xxx team members and this is what it includes and then provide a full list of items that's included'. Pause for 1-2 short seconds and ask if they have any question or if they are ready to proceed with the reservation.

Ask the client throughout the conversation to book the cleaning. Do not be pushy but ask for the booking because sometimes the client needs a little push to book.

When a client calls and simply goes straight to ask for a price say something like "Thank you so much for calling us. I'll be happy to provide you with that info and I just need to ask you some questions before doing so - is that ok? Then ask -how many bedrooms, # of bathrooms, what's the square footage approx., how soon do you need the cleaning to be done etc. you want to get as much info as possible before giving a potential cleaning range.

Another scenario is that if the price is too high for the first deep cleaning, then offer to 'cap the cleaning' - in this case, you'll need a list of priorities. Make sure client knows that depending on the cap rate - you may not be able to get thru the entire list.

Unlike other cleaning service in my market because we provide xx and xx and xx for our teams so in return our clients benefits by having loyal employees that understand you, our client, is the to be treated with respect of your home, your family, your belongings. This is extremely important because what happens often in the cleaning industry is that the turnover is nearly 400% - which causes a lot of issues to clients. At XYZ, the turnover is 25% per year and that number continues to decrease.

We have also won several awards including xxxxx and xxxxxx - these award and many others also gives the client the idea that we are a professional cleaning company, we are here for the long term and our goal is 100% client satisfaction.

If a client has determined that price is too much - you should simply say something like "I appreciate the insight and please do give us a call back if anything changes.".

Also - you can ask at the very end ---is there anything that I should have asked you that I didn't covered? Or is there anything else I may assist you with?

"Hello (username),

We are excited to have you on board. This is a quick email to introduce you to our team.

I've cc'ed our <u>customer service manager, xxxxx</u> here on this email. xxxxx will be creating your file, helping to coordinate logistics and so on. xxxxx is normally the 1st point of contact since she is in the office all day and I am always in between meetings.

<u>xxxxx</u> also cc'ed here is the Office Manager--either xxxx or xxxxx are available to answer invoice questions you may have. They will be in touch if they have any questions regarding servicing your account, invoices, etc.

Our <u>operations manager is xxxxxx</u>and you will probably see her or me during her inspections at your buildings. If at any time you would like to meet with us simply shoot us a quick email and we'll make sure we coordinate accordingly so Rosa or myself can meet with you during inspections.

Welcome to the xxxxxx community!
We are looking forward to working with you.
Best regards,
xxxxxx
Office: xxxxxxxxxx
Office Google # for Texting Only: xxxxxxx

If client does not accept proposal: SAMPLE

   ✓ Take out from post proposal email campaign and automatically assign to Enewsletter Campaign

If previous contact visits sites/ downloads whitepaper etc:

   ✓ Lets add them to the enewsletter but also lets dispatch a short auto email campaign
1 quick email with 1 link – if link is clicked a 2 email to be dispatched.

3rd email with a video and if video is watched then a 4 email asking for 10 mins phone call.

Perhaps video is a link to a landing page on site that host the video ---that would be better for

tracking purposes and to keep the client engage with 1 landing page that is cohesive to what

we've been emailing about.

CHAPTER 15 PRICE INCREASE

Thank you for your continued loyalty to xxxxxx. As you may now, every year the management

team meets to review each account in detail and the overall health of our company. Our year-

end review of our business expenses have revealed an increase in our overall operating

expenses. Almost without exception our benefit packages to our staff, suppliers, fuel,

insurance (workers comp, unemployment, auto insurance and general liability) **and labor costs**

have increased significantly due to the minimum wage hike etc. which includes travel time in

between jobs.

Your current monthly payment is $xxx per month which includes months with more than 4

weeks.

The updated price we can offer to continue providing you with the same service is $xxx per month. This price also includes months with more than 4 weeks. This price will be effective xxxxxx. Basically your cleaning per week cost would increase by only $xxx.

We greatly appreciate your continued business and look forward to providing you the same service you have grown to expect from us. We are locking this rate for 12 months. The next rate evaluation will be in January 2018.

Please reply <u>"Agree"</u> to this email so that we may update your file with the correct amount.

Thank you in advance!

Accordingly,

xxxxxx

Price Increase Follow Email

Dear,

We want to ensure that you received the email below. It's important for us to get your confirmation. Please respond "Agree" so that we may update your file accordingly.

Have a great weekend!

xxxxxxx

Some clients might respond that the price is too high, for that we have a template use it:

Dear xxxxxx,

Thank you for the insight. If you have a budget that you are working with, perhaps we can customize the service. For example, some rooms can be left out of the service.

We take great pride in providing the best service possible to our clients. Unlike a lot of the smaller companies and individual maids, we provide worker's compensation and general liability as well as bonuses, employee benefits and other overhead costs that affect our bottom line significantly.

Our prices are competitive with national service companies, such as The Maids, Merry Maids, and even individual maids such as Cida's Cleaning.

However, we understand that other companies can provide lower prices based on the minimal overheads.

You can definitely try them and if in the future you would like to reconsider our services, we would be delighted to hear from you.

Feel Free to our blog for more information on pricing and cleaning tips.

Warm Regards,

XXXXXXX

Sample Letter Introducing Company to Potential Client

Date

Dear Office Manager,

We service clients near your office in Lexington and we noticed xxx Construction's office is nearby. I wanted to take a moment to introduce our company and point you to our site which has lots of valuable content for your review (xxxxxxx). If you are experiencing any issues with your current cleaning company or are looking for a company that can truly become an extension of your team please give us a call or email us.

Here is a couple of some of our eguides:

How is your cleaning service an investment in your company's growth? an e-guide for managers responsible for hiring cleaning services. This e-guide will help you and your company save time, save money, achieve your objectives, and eliminate the mistakes that too many companies make when hiring a cleaning service.

Clean facilities are not just a cost. They generate revenue. This eGuide will provide you with research information to gain a greater understanding of the value of commercial cleaning and its corresponding impact on costs, profits and how it can even contribute in a positive way to lower your costs and increase your bottom line!

Our company, xxxxxx specializes in office, residential and commercial cleaning services, carpet cleaning and hard surface floor maintenance. We have clients who call us once a year and others that contract us for daily cleaning. whatever you needs may be, let's discuss and see if we could be a good fit for each other.

My direct tel #xxx-xxx-xxxx

Best regards,

xxxxxx

Title

Every Day in Every Way I am Becoming a Great Sales Person

Daily Actions DATE: _____

Read / Reply to Emails from 9am to 10am _____

Return Calls 9am -10am _____

***Pending Proposals to be done before Cold Calling

1 Hour cold-calling from 10am to 11am_____

2 letters per day -11 to 11:20am

- Letter 1 Sent to:

  _____

- Letter 2 sent to:

  _____

Break – til 11:45am

11:45 to 1pm - 10 emails per day to new contacts on linked or hatchbuck – Goal Achieved?

1:10pm to 1:30pm --- Place warm calls to 3 prospects per day – Goal Achieved? _____

1. Call

1:_____

2.Call

2:_____

3.Call

3:_____

1:45pm Ask for a referral 1 per day: **Who did we ask for a referral?**

_____

Give a referral 1 per week: Who did we recommend?_____

_____

2pm to 4pm – OPEN_____

Send an item of interest to 3 colleagues per week – which 3 people did we send something interesting?

- Colleague 1:_____
- Colleague 2:_____
- Colleague 3:_____

Client Meeting Agenda

Date: _____

Location:_____

_____

_____

Attendees:

_____

_____

_____

_____

1. Opening Comments
2. Items from Previous Meeting
3. Overall Satisfaction Assessment
4. Service Performance Review
a. Call Center
b. Quality Control Visit Reports
c. Personnel-Management Team
d. Other
5. Business Issues
a. Accounting
b. Safety
c. Security
d. Other
6. Other Items for Discussion

Action Items:

Item Due/Date/Status	Party Responsible
_____	_____
—	—
_____	_____
—	—
_____	_____
—	—
_____	_____
—	—

Next Meeting Date: _____

Good Email Follow Up Template

Hi xxxx,

Hope you had a good weekend. I didn't hear back from you on Friday so I wanted to follow up with you.

Does it make sense to dive into a deeper evaluation of Janitorial Services or should we put this on hold until end of summer?

If needed, I'm happy to introduce you to xxxx, our Client Experience Manager to help you get started.

xxxxxx

OFFICE / COMMERCIAL TELEPHONE QUESTIONNAIRE

Greetings! This is xxxxxxx speaking, may I ask how I can assist you? Great! Thank you for your interest in xxxxxxx!

I am just going to ask a few questions to ensure we are a good fit for each other. Is that ok?

Client's Full Name _____ Date: _____

Company's

Name:_____Title:_____
_____

May I ask, how did you find us? _____If referred by who?_____

What type of facility is it (office, apartment property, day care, bank, prof office, etc)?

_____

_____

_____

Full Address:

_____

_____

_____

Email: _____ Telephone:

_____

Do you require union-companies only? ___If yes, please let them know we are NON UNION if they say NO please proceed.

Service Needed: (daily, twice per week, weekly, biweekly, every four weeks, etc)?

- Regular Cleaning _____If so, what frequency are you interested in? Daily, 2 per week, weekly, biweekly, etc_____and what hours work best for you?_____
- One time Deep Cleaning ONLY_____
- Carpet Cleaning _____
- Strip & Wax

_____

- Other_____

_____

_____

Do you currently have an outsourced cleaning service or is the cleaning currently done inhouse?

If present cleaning company– may I ask, why are you looking to replace them?

_____

_____

In order to give you an accurate quote we would need to schedule an on-site visitation so one of our managers can take a look at the space. An on-site is an extremely important, one time process to capture intricate details of the site, understand special customer needs and develop a trustworthy relationship.

Help us provide you with a fair and accurate proposal for our janitorial services. Place client on hold for one second and see what day manager is available for on site based on clients availability....then confirm with client if xxxx at xxx works for you to meet with us.

Before I let you go, may I ask if you have a formal RFP or written specifications you can share with us? If yes ---please email them to us to info@xxxxxx.com

Thank you for your time, we look forward to seeing you on xxxxxxxxxxxx at xxxxxxxxxx.

Hi xxxxx how are you today? Do you have a minute to chat? This is xxxxxxx from xxxx company and I am calling because we've noticed that lately we seem to be more of headache than a solution to you. It's for this reason that we've decided that it would be best for another service to provide you with your cleaning needs. Would you like for me to email you a few recommendations? I am confirming via this call that all future services have been cancelled in our system and your credit card on file will be deleted and no longer charged. I want to thank you for your support throughout the years and i wish you the best of luck. Thank you very much!

Make sure to email the recommendations if client says yes!

CHAPTER 16 - QUOTE REQUEST PROCESS MAP SAMPLE ONLY

1)   Quote Received –Auto email campaign for 5 weeks to get us to schedule an onsite visitation.

2)   A phone call to request on site (xxxx) – if no answer an Email sent back requesting an onsite.

a.   Perhaps the email can have a link to a video or quick 1 pager "Why Working with a Legitimate Company Matters". Or Why xxxxxx May be the best choice and how to find out?

3)   If email is not answered – a 2nd email sent to follow up

4)   On site scheduled –

a.   Put together the proposal.

b.   Proposal sent - (reminders sent weekly)

d.   xxxx to add client to the Scheduling platform with notes and specific date for the onsite and all contact info.

a.   Take reminder off when client lets us know they are ready to proceed or have move on to another cleaning company.

b.   If proposal sent – take out from initial auto email and set them up for a 'client conversion email campaign' – email should be simple – more personal and with 1 link to a white paper / eguide etc –

     i.   one email with 'I thought this would be beneficial for you",

     ii.   another email with 'I would like to set up a time to chat for a couple of mins to go over any questions you may have or simply chat about where in the process of deciding are you…

     iii.   and then another email with –"Hi xxx, I am just checking in since we haven't heard from you…and if they do talk with us then go into another set of emails – every 5 days perhaps –send a link to a video, or to a whitepaper or ?

c.   1 email with a video clip – 30 seconds clip introducing the office staff and how we can be of service –followed with list of contact info. xxxx at xxx@xxxx.com for general questions / feedback etc – tel # and letting them know that invoices are coming from which email and if check –made payable to xxxxx and if CC they can also pre pay to get x% off .

When a proposal is sent – include that proposal on the notes on CRM / Hatchbuck so if client calls anyone of us can answer any questions -

If client accepts the proposal:

1)   Send email – welcoming client to the 'Family'.

a.   And remove from auto campaigns – add to Enewsletter Sign up only.

b.   Then forward proposal notes to office staff setting up new customer file.

c.   xxxxx to make work order in the Scheduling program

d.   Confirm 'the prorated rate if applicable' and information added to Qbooks accordingly.

e.   Decide which employee will be assigned to the account

f.   Update payroll if needed for that assigned employee to the account

2)   Follow up immediately after 1st cleaning to ensure satisfaction –then every 3 months schedule.   Once per week –Supervisor to do 1 inspection in each account to ensure cleaners are doing a good job – schedule on scheduling program.

b.   Put an alarm on google to send an alert – review payroll margins for the account at the 1 week mark and then every 4 months to ensure profitability of the account.

If client doesn't accept Proposal:

1)   Take out from "Client conversion email" campaign and add to "Previously Interested On Site Received" campaign –this campaign should be sent every 2 months to remind clients we are the real experts – email including "Having challenges with your current cleaner – eguide", "updates from the company about video clips, etc.

2)   Send questionnaire to figure out why they didn't pick us – questionnaire needs to be developed – we want to find out if the decision was based on value proposition, price, confusions, etc.

Xxxxxx Process Map WHEN Leads CALLS (NO EMAIL):

1)   Potential Client calls to inquire about service / rates

2)   xxxx speaks to Client and asks all the question on the Quote Request – and xxx schedules an onsite with client for manager.

a.   Set up the client on CRM to start the 'client conversion email'

3)   On site scheduled – do on site with client

a.   Put together the proposal.

b.   Send proposal.

c.   Add client to the scheduling program with notes and specific date for the onsite and all contact info.

4)   Within 24 hrs check that client proposal was received and set up weekly email reminders for the client.

a.   Take reminder off when client lets us know they are ready to proceed or have move on to another cleaning company.

b.   If proposal sent – take out from initial auto email and set them up for a 'client conversion email campaign' – email should be simple – more personal and with 1 link to a white paper / eguide etc –

     i.   one email with 'I thought this would be beneficial for you",

ii.   another email with 'I would like to set up a time to chat for a couple of mins to go over any questions you may have or simply chat about where in the process of deciding are you...

iii.   and then another email with –"Hi xxx, I am just checking in since we haven't heard from you...and if they do talk with us then go into another set of emails – every 5 days perhaps –send a link to a video, or to a whitepaper or ?

c.   1 email with a video clip – 30 seconds clip introducing the office staff and how we can be of service –followed with list of contact info. xxxxx at xxxx@xxxxx for general questions / feedback etc – tel # and letting them know that invoices are coming from which email and if check –made payable to xxxx and if CC they can also pre pay to get xxx% off – or maybe we can use this content on an initial email right after the proposal or before the proposal to ensure they know and it's easy for them to do biz with us.

d.   When a proposal is sent – include that proposal on the notes on CRM so if client calls anyone of us can answer any questions -

Some additional content ideas / Topics:

·   Safety and Security – How xxxx handles the safety of your offices / residential homes etc.

·   Top 5 Security Concerns for Property Managers

·   10 must haves for an effective Request for Proposal template to ensure you meet with the 'right' contractors for the job?

Trigger: Proposal Request Received

- New Contact Record created in CRM
- Task / Alert (xx): Proposal request, action needed
- Activity (xxxxx): request on-site visit (change status based on response)
- Email Series: xxxx Introduction (3-parts)

Trigger: On-Site Meeting Scheduled

- Activity (xxx): Schedule meeting date with client
- Email Series: Client conversion campaign (4-parts)
- Task (xxx): Add client to the Schedule with notes and specific date for the onsite and all contact info.
- Task (xx): Within 24 hrs check that echosign proposal was viewed
- Task (xx): Send weekly reminder to the client (for how many weeks?)

Trigger: On-Site Meeting Declined (See Trigger: Opportunity Status = Closed Lost)

Trigger: On-Site Meeting Conducted/Proposal Requested:

- Activity (xx): Create and deliver proposal immediately following on-site visit

Trigger: Proposal Delivered

- Create New Opportunity: Include dollar value, and related metrics
- Send Email Template: Proposal was delivered today via Echosign
  - Opportunity Record Note: Proposal was delivered
- Recurring Task (xxx): Call 48 hours after delivery, and every 48 hours after for 8 days

Trigger: Lead Score Increase / Decrease (based on email opens, click-thrus, web visits, etc)

- Task/Alert (xx): Score reaches threshold, contact prospect via phone

Trigger: Proposal Signed through Echosign

- Update Contact Status - from prospect to customer
- Send Email Template: 'Welcome to the Family'
- Stop all pre-sales email campaigns
- Add to e-newsletter signup
- Alert / Task (xx): Proposal was signed, see related tasks
- Task (xx): Make work order in Scheduling Manager
- Task (xx): Confirm 'the prorated rate if applicable'

- Task (xx): send customer info to Quickbooks
- Task (xx): Assign employee to the account

Trigger: Employee assigned to account

- Task (xx): Update payroll if needed for that assigned employee to the account
- Task (xx): Confirm payroll adjustments
- Activity: xx training scheduled
- Task (xxx): Schedule first-cleaning follow-up
- Task (xx): Setup recurring task (every-3-months) email client to review account and setup meeting
- Task (xx): Setup once-per-week inspections in the Scheduling Manager
- Activity (xx): Initial payroll margin review 1 week after 1st cleaning
- Activity (): Recurring profitability review (every 4 months)

Trigger: Opportunity Status = Closed Lost

- Delete follow up tasks
- Stop email campaigns
- Start email campaign: "Previously Interested, Site Visited" Every 2 months for _____
- Send survey
- Recycle lead (define follow up further)

CRM Requirements:

- Automation for creating follow-up tasks
- Creating tasks from email activity
- Notifications for new tasks, or when tasks are due
- Triggers for sending contact data to Quickbooks
- Create repeating tasks: http://goo.gl/f88imB
- Task & note templates?
- Ability to create shared tasks

Email campaigns:

- Email Series - On-Site Scheduled/Conducted: Why choose xxxxxx
- Email Series – No On-Site Conducted: Why didn't you choose xxxx?
- Email Series - Client conversion campaign (3-parts?)
- Recycle Campaign (Site Visited) – deliver every 2 months:
  - remind clients we are the real experts – email including "Having challenges with

your current cleaner – eguide", "updates from the company about video clips, etc.

- Closed-Lost Survey: Why they didn't pick us - based on value proposition, price, confusions, etc.
- Email: Safety and Security – How XYZ handles the safety of your offices / residential homes etc.
- Email: Top 5 Security Concerns for Property Managers
- Email: 10 must haves for an effective Request for Proposal template to ensure you meet with the 'right' contractors for the job?

I.   Pre-employment job application

II.   Orientation / Full background Report completed

_____(Date of Completion) - copy of social security / id, license etc needed prior to background check.

A.   Must watch corresponding videos depending on position --residential cleaning video, commercial videos, etc.

Explain pay-day calendar – and amount employee will get paid (we pay weekly on Fridays).

B.   Emphasize the following in the Employee Policy Manual:

1. Attendance and punctuality

a.   Must call in 3 hours prior to shift if not going to work.

b.   Must call if going to be late.
No drugs or alcohol allowed ever

2. Hours and Location - advise that hours and location of job may change depending on position.

3. Training - advise that employees may be re-trained for other jobs.

4. Uniforms - advise uniform must be worn at all times. Proper shoes must be worn at all times --no open toes or open hill allowed.

5. Employee conduct

   a.   Point out that rules that when broken result in written or oral discipline.

   b.   Point out that rules that when broken result in

         immediate termination such as showing up under the influence of drugs or alcohol, being physical with a client or team member

6. Resignations - advise that we require at least two weeks notice when possible.

7. Review hair, jewelry, nail, shoes expectations as well as communication requirements with team mates.

8. Attendance –2 weeks if needs a day off for appointments etc and must wait to hear that it's possible to take day off.

9. Vacation Policy- advise full-time employees receive vacation pay based on the number of hours worked.

10. Breaks - advise employees working 6 hours or more, receive 30 minute break and how they can take their lunch break (unpaid).

11. Group insurance - advise full-time employees are eligible for group insurance after 90 days of employment.. Company pays for 50% of the employee's monthly premium.

12. Holiday Policy – advise full-time employees are paid for listed holidays.

C.   Employee Work Ethic and Safety Policy Packet

1. Advise them of "No Theft" Allowed

2. Advise them of xxxxxx Team Work Expectations.

3. Advise them of Rubber Glove and Eye Protection Policy.

4. Advise them of Hazard Communication Training.

5. Advise them of Lifting Policy --lifting items with 2 people, dragging items that can damage floors is not allowed.

6. Advise them of Sexual Harassment Policy

***& office google # as well as regular phone number --which # to use based on situation.

D. Have employee read and verify that all blanks are filled and that signature of employee and xxxxxxx Representative/Trainer is complete.

E. Receipt and Acknowledgment Form - have employee complete and verify that all blanks are filled with appropriate checks, initials and signatures.

F. Medical Review - have employee complete and verify that all blanks are filled with appropriate checks, initials and signatures.

G.   W4 - have employee complete and verify that # of exemptions are documented with signature and date.

H.   I9 - have employee complete top portion, then we fill out bottom with identification they provide according to I9 requirements.

I.   Uniform - provide employee with work shirt. Full-time = 2;

Part-time = 1. If they want, they may purchase extras polos or t-shirts from the company

J.   Badge - provide employee with badge. drivers must have their driving license at all times.

K.   Uniform Receipt Acknowledgment Form - have employee complete.

L.   Post-Hire Assignment Form-we complete, then have employee sign & date.

M.   Copies - make copies of:

     1.   Identification provided by employee (Soc. Sec. Card, Green Card, Driver's License, Passport,

etc.)

    2. Post-Hire Assignment Form - give copy to employee, we keep original.

    3. Uniform Receipt Acknowledgment Form - give copy to employee, we keep original.

N.   Be sure employee knows when, where & to whom they are to report for work.

Write this on their copy of the Post-Hire Assignment Form.

III.   When all is completed:

A.   Employee should SIGN / and fully understand the following: When finished provide all copies to Payroll.

    1. Employee Policy Manual / Pay Day Calendar

    2. Copy of employee confidentiality and non-compete agreement.

    3. Timekeeping Procedures

    4. Uniform Forms & Other company policies

    5. Prey-employment Job Application

6. W4 / I9

7. Health Insurance forms, other forms?

8. Copies of identification / green card, social security, license, etc.

Completed by: _____

Date: _____

Fecha:_____ **Nombre Del**

Empleado:_____

El empleado indicado anteriormente ha trabajado para la compañía durante _____. Por lo tanto, este empleado debe saber cuáles son las normas que esperamos de él / ella con el fin de proporcionar a nuestros clientes una experiencia de limpieza verdaderamente excepcional. Desafortunadamente este empleado no se está realizando a la altura. La falta de rendimiento adecuado crea no sólo las quejas de los clientes, sino también improductiva ya que otros miembros del equipo deben de compensar la falta de actuación de este empleado. Las siguientes áreas han sido inspeccionadas y se han encontrado deficiencias importantes en el trabajo.

Areas de Deficiencias incluyen pero no son limitadas a:

1-_____

2-_____

3-_____

Este es un aviso por escrito de que debe de mejorar su calidad de rendiemiento immediatamente.

Firma del Empleado:_____Fecha:_____

Firma del Jefe:_____Fecha:_____

The employed indicated above has been working for the company for _____. Therefore, this employee should know what standards we expect from him/her in order to provide our clients with a truly 5 star cleaning experience. Unfortunately this employee is not performing up to standards. The lack of proper performance creates not only complaints from clients but also it its unproductive since other team members need to work order to compensate the lack of performance from this employee. The following areas have been inspected and we have found major deficiencies in the work.

1-_____

2-_____

3-_____

This is a written warning due to poor performance. You must improve your performance quality immediately.

Employee's Signature:_____Date:_____

Manager's Signature:_____Date:_____

1.   Send Invoice the day of the cleaning if we don't have cc on file

2.   Send invoice and PayPal especially if we don't know the client's preference —once we know the clients preference make sure we follow it

3.   3 days later ---email the client and let the client know invoice is pending ---all residential cleanings are due the day (same day of cleaning latest 48 hrs) so the process should be clear – unless it's Friday

4.   In 7 days call / text the client

5.   In 12 days When client calls to pay ask to avoid future inconveniences if client wants to provide a cc for future payments —a nice message template should be draft for Liz to use---we have to be polite at all times but we need the payment

6.   In 15 days xxxx to give a list of clients that we need to be more 'forceful' with ---Liz needs to start the Persistent Process below with an official letter etc –

7.   In 30 days –Email a letter to the client's ---OFFICIAL letter #1

8.   In 35 days make a 2nd call to the client asking for payment –again –draft the phone call so xxxx uses 1 template for phone calls and other one for text and one for the letters ---we have to be polite but persistent.

9.   In 40 days –let client know services will be put on hold if payment is not received

10.   In 60 days – account will be sent to collection agency –goal is to NEVER EVER NEVER GET TO THIS POINT and there will be extra fees associated with this process –whatever we discussed in the past --

Create standard collection letters and call scripts to support this process. The message should be brief and to the point:

> *Thank you for your business*
>
> *Your account is now past due*
>
> *Let us know if there is a problem or error*
>
> *Otherwise, please remit the amount due*
>
> *Thank you again for your business*

CHAPTER 19 - HIRING / FIRING / DISCIPLINARY ACTION FOR STAFF MEMBERS

When a position becomes available. The first group of people to know the position is now available is your entire current staff. Let all employees know that you are hiring and for what position. If the employee is required to drive, make sure to let the employees know. They are likely the #1 to find good reliable employees. You can even give them $100 after 3 months of a new hire that has been referred by them.

You may also post it in newspapers - make sure to have a Spanish and English ad. The best ads are the ones that have the hourly rate and that mention that the company provides the vehicles. Lots of potential employees may be able to work but are afraid they need to provide their own vehicles since many other cleaning companies requires their staff to provide their own vehicles. So this is a huge plus for new potential employees.

When interviewing make sure to schedule the interview for when you are alert and ready to rock! Do not book interviews first thing in the morning when arriving to the office or just before going home for the day. At those times you are either too busy trying to figure out what's going on for the day or too tired to ask the best questions.

When interviewing make sure to ask a lot of open ended questions especially as it related to the person's health, skills as it relates to conversation, teamwork, and attitude? It is okay to hire someone that has never cleaned before. But it is not okay to hire someone that has a poor attitude, has knee, back, arm / leg problems because this is a very physical job. An employee that has mental health related to anxiety may also be a problem if the person has to drive a vehicle so the best way to find out without getting into a lawsuit is to ask - "how do you work with others? Have you ever had issues with another employee in your shift? How do you handle stress? Have you ever have an argument with another team member and why? Ask a lot of "have you ever" questions to determine the person's attitude toward teamwork.

Make sure to set clear expectations during the interview of what's allowed and what isn't allowed at the company as it relates to teamwork and respect. This is a position that requires a lot of teamwork, mutual respect and good communication while working at the job sites.

Tips when Firing an Employee:

You may often need to fire employees or ask them to resign. If at all possible is best if the employee signs a form indicating that they are resigning. This will help if your employee ends up going to unemployment. We had the Unemployment Dept contact us years after an employee has left the company so it's imperative to keep all employees files forever.

#1 - always have a witness with you (a manager or supervisor) to witness the conversation.

#2 - if the employee is aggressive you may need to have a male in the room as well ready to jump in if needed.

#3 - never start the conversation with "What happened" - start the conversation with "Marie - we are here today because unfortunately we do not longer fit we are a good fit for each other. Therefore i am kindly asking you to resign."

#4 - if the employee refuses to resign - say "Unfortunately, even if you do not want to sign the termination letter, please know that you are no longer effective as of today working for Company xyz. This is your last check for services rendered. We need your uniform back by xxxx date please. Thank you for your services and we wish you the best of luck.

When doing any training or discussing employee performance or customer complaints or other issues that an employee must address and avoid in the future, make sure to document it. It's critical to date the form, have the employee sign and have a manager sign that the conversation occurred and that the employee knows what actions must be improved immediately.

If you are discussing something that you do not think requires an employee to sign, you can still write it up and sign it with the date you spoke with the employee. Keep employee files up to date so when something serious comes up or something has happened more than once you can refer to the file and show the employee when you last discussed the situation and that this is now a written warning since you had already given them a verbal warning and the situation did not improve. Ensure employee knows that any further issues depending on the seriousness of the matter may result in suspension including up to termination.

There are times when an employee with bad attitude can have an effect on the entire team. When this happens you have to act quickly and discuss the employee's performance and let this person know that anything else will result in immediate termination as you do not allow bad / poor attitude towards clients or other employees in the company. This is non-negotiable! We've been thru this a couple of times with employees that have affected everyone's productivity for weeks and even months and we learned the hard way that's best to pay unemployment for such employee and be short-staffed than to keep someone that's seriously affecting your team! Do not let it happen. The first time there is an issue address it, the 2nd time give a written warning, the 3rd time terminate the employee.

We have worked with employees that are terrible cleaners and have helped them become great cleaners but someone with a poor attitude is extremely hard to change. The cost to change someone's attitude is extremely expensive to us and therefore we do not allow it.

During the interview process, we let the employee know that a background must be done before moving forward with the hiring process. In order to do so, 2 forms of id such a license or state ID card and social must be provided. If you are hiring a maid specialist to drive as well, their license must be over 2 years old to avoid premium charges and his/her record must be in good standing. Let the employee know that even though you hire then, once the background check is provided to us, if we find issues we may not be able to keep them. It's important for you to have this in writing and explain it to the employee to avoid lawsuits, etc.

The background check must include sexual offenders - do not hire anyone that has criminal issues related to theft, sexual offenses, etc as your staff is to clean homes and buildings where clients live or work.

Chapter 20 - Account Receivables Process for Residential Clients

1. Send Invoice the day of the cleaning if we don't have cc on file and if client does not pay by check
   a. Send quickbook invoice and PayPal invoice especially if we don't know the client's preference —once we know the clients preference make sure we follow it
   b. Deep Cleans must be sent both quickbooks and PayPal unless client specifies how they will pay

2. Next business day AFTER invoice has been sent - call client to request payment
   a. No answer → leave voice message
   b. If cannot leave voice message text the client

3. (4 days from sending invoice) 3 days later ---Email #1
   a. **Dear xxxx,**

      This is a friendly reminder that the attached invoice is now due. Prompt payment is greatly appreciated.

      Thank you for your business.

      Warm Regards,

      xxxxx

4. (7 days past due) 3 days later call / text the client –
   a. TEXT:
      i. This is a friendly reminder that your invoice in the amount of $$$ for cleaning services on DATE is now past due. Please call us to process payment or visit us online to pay via PayPal. Thank you, Company xyz.

        ii.

   b. CALL:

        i.   Good Morning/ Good Afternoon (client name), this is Liz from Company xyz. How are you today? I am calling to request payment for the cleaning services provided on xxxx. The total due is xxxx. We accept all major credit cards over the phone. Would you like to process payment now? Or is there a better time to call you? We also accept PayPal online.

        ii.   Voice Message: Good Morning/ Good Afternoon (client name), this is xxx from Company xyz. I am calling to request payment for the cleaning services provided on xxxx. The total due is xxxx. We emailed you a copy of your invoice a few days ago. We accept all major credit cards over the phone. We also accept PayPal online. Please call us at 617-553-1393 to process payment or if you have any questions.

5. (10 days past due) 3 days later, Email #2

   a. **Dear xxxx,**

     This is a friendly reminder that the attached invoice is now past due. Prompt payment is greatly appreciated.

     We accept credit cards over the phone and PayPal online.

     Thank you for your business.

     Warm Regards,

     xxxxx

6. (13 days past due) - 3 days later text / call #2

   a. CALL

        i.   Good Morning/ Good Afternoon (client name), this is Liz from Company xyz. How are you? I am calling to request payment for the cleaning services provided on xxxx. The total due is xxxx. We accept all major credit cards over the phone. Would you like to process payment now? Or is there a better time to call you? We also accept PayPal online

    ii.   Voice Message: Good Morning/ Good Afternoon (client name), this is Liz from Company xyz. I am calling to request payment for the cleaning services provided on xxxx. The total due is xxxx. We emailed you a copy of your invoice a few days ago. We accept all major credit cards over the phone. We also accept PayPal online. Please call us at xxxxxxxto process payment or if you have any questions.

    b. TEXT:

        i.   This is a friendly reminder that your balance of xxxx is now past due. Please call us to process a credit card payment or visit us at xxxxx.com to process a PayPal payment. Thank you! - Company xyz

7. (16 days past due) - 3 days later Email #3

    a. **Dear xxxx,**

        We understand that our clients are quite busy. This is a friendly reminder that the balance on your account remains unpaid. Your invoice is now over 15 days past due.

        To avoid a late fee charge of $25, please remit payment within the next 48 hours. We accept credit cards over the phone and PayPal online.

        Prompt payment is greatly appreciated.
        Thank you for your business.

        Warm Regards,
        xxxxxx

8. (19 days past due)- 3 days apply the $25 late fee and text /call #3

    a. TEXT:

        i.   A late fee of $25 has been applied to your invoice. Your amount of $xxxx is now due. Please call us to process payment or visit us online to pay via PayPal. Thank you, xxxxxxx.

b.   Good Morning/ Good Afternoon (client name), this is xxxxx from xxxx xxx. How are you? I am calling to request payment for the cleaning services provided on xxxx. The total due is xxxx. We accept all major credit cards over the phone. Would you like to process payment now? Or is there a better time to call you? We also accept PayPal online

c.   Voice Message: Good Morning/ Good Afternoon (client name), this is xxx from xxxxxxx. I am calling to request payment for the cleaning services provided on xxxx. The total due is xxxx. We emailed you a copy of your invoice a few days ago. We accept all major credit cards over the phone. We also accept PayPal online. Please call us at xxxxxxxx to process payment or if you have any questions.

9. (22 days past due)- 3 days later Email #4 and USPS mail #1 along with invoice

a. Dear xxxx,

Your attached invoice is now over 21 days past due. Our records indicate that we have not received your payment which was due on xxxxx. A late fee of $25 has been applied.

We hope this was just an oversight and you will be able to remit payment immediately.

Prompt payment is greatly appreciated. We accept PayPal online and credit cards payments over the phone.

Thank you for your business.

Warm Regards,

10. (30 days past due)

a. Regular Client

i.   Service will be put on hold until payment is received.

ii. **Dear xxxx,**

Your attached invoice is now over 30 days past due.

We regret to inform you that your services have been placed on hold until we receive full amount due.

If there is an error on our part and payment has been made, please contact us immediately so that the matter can be rectified.

Prompt attention to this matter is greatly appreciated.

Yours Truly,

xxxxx

b. Deep Clean/ On Call
   i. Email #5 / mail #2
   ii. **Dear xxxx,**

Your attached invoice is now over 30 days past due. Our records indicate that we have not received your payment which was due on xxxxx. A late fee of $25 has been applied.

As it has not been possible to resolve this matter, we regret to advise that unless payment is received by xxxx at 3pm this invoice will be turned over to our debt collection agency.

If there is an error on our part and payment has been made, please contact us immediately so that the matter can be rectified.

Prompt payment is greatly appreciated.

Warm Regards,

xxxxx

11. (35 days past due) - NT Send Deep Clean/ One Time clients to collections if payment has not been received

12. (40 days past due)
    a. If Regular client has not paid, send email #5, mail #2 about collections
        i. Give them 4 business day to make payment or be sent to collections

13. (45 days past due)
    a. NT Submit regular client to Collections

DIFFERENT THAN residential

Monthly Clients:

1. Invoice sent on the 1st Monday of the month, due on the 7th of the next month
   a. Client who pay per visit, must be emailed on the day of service, invoice due Net 30
2. On the 4th of every month (or Friday before if the 4th falls on the weekend), Liz to send reminder through Quickbooks to all commercial clients who have not paid.
   a. Dear xxxx,

   This is a friendly reminder that the attached invoice is due in x days. Prompt payment is greatly appreciated.

   Thank you for your business.

   Warm Regards,

   xxxxxx

3. 3 days after payment is due - send an updated reminder indicating payment is now past due.
   a. Dear xxxx,

   Your attached invoice is now xxx days past due. Prompt payment is greatly appreciated.

   If you prefer to have your invoices automatically paid, we are happy to email you a credit card authorization form via EchoSign.

Warm Regards,

xxxxx

4. (10 days after payment is due) 7 days from the last email → Liz to call the client and ask if there's anything we can do to make it easy to collect payment now or in the future? Let them know we accept credit card payments and or they can set up online bill pay with their bank if their bank offers it

5. (17 days after payment is due) 7 days after the call → Send email #2
   a. Dear xxxx,

   Your attached invoice is now xxx days past due. Prompt payment is greatly appreciated.

   If you prefer to have your invoices automatically paid, we are happy to email you a credit card authorization form via EchoSign.

   We would appreciate an update on the payment status.

   Warm Regards,

   xxxxx

6. (24 days past due) 7 days after email #2, send 1st friendly letter via regular usps mail
   a. Dear xxxx,

   Your attached invoice is now past due. Prompt payment is greatly appreciated.

   If you prefer to have your invoices automatically paid, we are happy to email you a credit card authorization form via EchoSign.

   Warm Regards,

   xxxxxx

7. (30 days past due) Notify manager/s to review and decide how to proceed

8. 45 days past due - 2nd letter via USPS
9. 60 days past due- Apply past due fee, mail letter and invoice showing new charges
   a. - Late fee for payments 60 days past due -
      what is this fee? 3%
      i. what if the client declines to pay it? We would need to have a mgt team meeting to review what to do with the client
10. 75 days past due apply late fee? - Final letter via email and mail about sending it to collections
11. 90 days past due submit to collections

Create standard collection letters and call scripts to support this process. The message should be brief and to the point:

WHAT IS THE PURPOSE OF THIS PAYABLE LIST?

✓ Use a simple ledgent system to enter the payment and put a color we know means account payable on google calendar and a $ sign before the name of the account that needs to be paid —we need a system that it's easy to know what we doing and how much we are paying to that account.

✓ xxxxx to send an email to new clients who don't have a credit card on file when they sign up for service and ask if they want to do so ---this simple email can be quite helpful

Dear xxxx,

We are very excited to start a work relationship with you and your organization.

As I am preparing your account for billing, I want to inform you that we offer a 1% discount for client who wish to prepay services with check payments at the beginning of the month. If you would like to take advantage of this discount, please note that we can only accept check payments. You can set up automatic payments with your bank or with your accounts payable representative.

If you do not wish to prepay the service, you will receive invoices on the first Monday of the month and payment is due on the 7th day of the next month. For example, On June 6th invoices for June services will be emailed and payments are due by July 7th.

We offer the option to provide a credit card for us to charge automatically on your day of preference or on the 1st day of the month. If you would like to receive the authorization form, let us know and we will email it to you.

If invoices are to be emailed to another person other than yourself, please provide us the person's name and email address. Please note that invoices will come from xxxxxxx@xxxxx.com. If invoices must be mailed, please let us know.

Thank you for choosing xxxxxxx We look forward to a lasting work relationship.

Warm Regards,

xxxxxx

CHAPTER 22 - CUSTOMER COMPLAINT ABOUT NOT SPENDING ENOUGH TIME IN CLIENT'S HOME

Whether you call or email the client, you have to make sure that your operational process and how you market your business reflect how your cleaners work. If the cleaners are working based on the hour, the clients will pay attention to that, if you pay the cleaners by commission and client doesn't know how long the cleaners will spend in their homes be ready to explain to the client that you train your staff to work effectively and efficiently to minimize times in the home without affecting the actual cleaning quality. Some clients even check their alarms to see how long you take in their homes especially if they are aware that you are charging them by the hour.

Also if the clients expect 1, 2, 3, or 4 cleaners and they notice you have sent more or less they may question you about that so make sure when you sign up new clients that they know how many people you dispatch and what happens if some of your staff calls sick or goes on vacation. See the Cleaning Specifications Agreement Email and the Welcome Page to see more on this topic.

Dear xxxx,
We truly appreciate your feedback.
On your next cleaning we will schedule a deep clean of your house to ensure the premise is brought to our cleaning standards. A training manager will visit to inspect the premise and review the bed situation with the team.
On recurring services, we will monitor the time being spent to ensure that the maids are spending sufficient time to maintain your home and the manager will inspect from time to time.
If after any service, the maids fail to provide a proper service, feel free to let us know and we will dispatch them to re-clean the areas in question.
Our manager will review with the team to ensure they give your home the proper care it deserves.
We truly apologize for the inconveniences our team has caused.
Best regards,

xxxxxx

CHAPTER 23 - SUPPLIERS / VENDOR RELATIONSHIPS

This is a quick topic to discuss but also an important one. You may start purchasing your supplies and equipment from Amazon, Home Depot or some other local supplier but as soon as you can you need to request meetings with local janitorial suppliers to learn more about their products, request samples on floor cleaning, air fresheners, bathroom mildew cleaners, and whatever else you may need. Just because you are small does not mean you have to be shy, actually it's the perfect way to start a relationship with suppliers. Show them that you are a professional in the business and you plan to grow / expand your services and you need a supplier you can trust.

Once you get their quotes on the products and equipment requested, negotiate it. Simple let them know that you were hoping for better pricing and you hope they can evaluate their quote once more. Make sure you are negotiating with at least 2-3 suppliers. We had one major supplier and 2 backup suppliers for floor equipment and floor chemicals. Our main supplier was good for everyday things but our backup suppliers were excellent for major janitorial floor chemicals so we depended on a couple of suppliers at all times.

Make sure to keep records and copy of all emails with the pricing. There are times when their prices go up and you won't notice because they will not take the time to let you know. Some suppliers (and perhaps all of them) will update their prices online and you will never notice unless every time you order you cross references your original list. This happened to us several times and each time I went back to our suppliers and asked them to reduce the price again to match my initial rate. Of course some of their prices may go up and they won't be able to reduce their prices but in 7 years only once for a specific trash bag we couldn't negotiate the cost of those heavy duty liners.

I recommend keeping a google spreadsheet and a hard copy of the spreadsheet as well. Every time you place an order make sure to cross reference and keep the records of all your orders by using a purchase order number sequence in place. For example, your first order would be PO which is short for Purchase Order #1, then PO #2, and so on. Eventually over the years you can get to over 500+ purchase orders. The more organized you are the easier its to track your spending per month, per year and compare janitorial supplies and equipment over the years. For us, our janitorial supplies and equipment were 1.6% to 3% of revenues. The more we grew the lower the janitorial expenses got. Initially the cost were about 3% of revenues for supplies and equipment because we were not negotiating price often, we were buying from a local supplier and we didn't use an efficient dispensing system. Once we decided to use a dispensing system and change our supplies to decrease costs we saw a difference immediately. We also order vacuums from our suppliers instead of buying them from local supplier. We spent weeks looking for the right suppliers and meeting different vendors and attending trade shows to develop the right relationships.

As you grow and are asked by your clients, especially if you are in the commercial industry, to provide store equipment in the client's location you must keep a spreadsheet and a note on your Customer Relationship Management software of where you have equipment. I've seen so many cleaning companies (include large cleaning companies) that are replaced by us and their equipment is left behind! Your notes should be clear and if a client cancels you must place an alarm on your software to pick up your equipment and supplies/chemicals on the last day of service. We have accounts that have over $7,000 and more on floor equipment and if they cancel or reduce service and those machines do not need to be left in the client's location we remove them to our office so we can use those equipment in other client's location.

A last minute note is to remember ---every year do an analysis and make sure you meet with your supplier and check in. We had very good relationships with our supplier and meet every quarter just to check in but if you can't just get it done at least once a year. Ask them to invoice you instead of paying every time you order with a debit or credit card. This helps you by giving you 30 days extra to pay for expenses. Whenever you can make sure your suppliers and vendors give you 30 days to pay them so you have some breathing room especially because our clients also take 30 or even more days to pay us so we have to have some breathing room and this is one way to do so. Do not pay them late though you need the suppliers on your side and they have to see you as a great client. Whenever possible refer them as well and make sure your main salesperson knows you are referring them.

Actually just one more note: Another way to make extra money is to offer your commercial clients the option for you to purchase their cleaning supplies, trash liners and paper goods and charge then a specific percentage for the service. We charged 15% fee of the total of each bill. Over the years and if you have large accounts this is a good chunk of money for ordering supplies. You still have to work to earn this money by having your staff request the right quantities at the right time so your clients don't have too much inventory on hand unnecessarily. Also make sure you negotiate, negotiate and negotiate on behalf of your client. We had a property manager get on my back because we were paying way too much for trash liners. He was right, once I looked at his complained and negotiate the price for the specific liners, i realized we were paying almost 3 times as much just because someone i failed to negotiate pricing on those liners. I was very upset with myself for failing the client. We kept the client and they were very understanding but another client may not have been so understanding and may have thought we were negligent on purpose.

If you don't have a scheduling platform make sure to decide first what is it that you need and must have, would like and would be really nice to have before you decide on a plan. Create a google sheet or excel and write down all the tasks/ features / functionality you desire from your scheduling platform. Place all the functionalities on the column a, then column b thru f add the names of the scheduling platforms that – then place an x or check mark on the companies that support the specific functions you need.

Here is a sample:

Scheduling / Booking Platform for Cleaning Company Requirements							
Important Features	Thoughtful Systems	Service Autopilot	Service CEO	http://maideasysoftware.com	Jobber.com	CleanTelligent	ZenMaid
advanced days we want --2 or 3 days or							
month, # of special projects, etc -sales and							
Should synch with Quickbooks (IDEALLY)							
'overview of specific day' so we can quickly							
systems all the data and import to new							
thoughtful systems from beginning to now --							
specific date, for biweekly, every 3,4,5 or 6							
If it fails, would the update be automatic?							
things to do- Alarm system for following up							
well from software							
ones are closer when scheduling to make it							
know who the location manager is --may be							
Team Member X Notes							
date per team as we do now in SM							
residential							
all work order in that job scheduled							
automatically when scheduling							
Must provide start time and end time							
Must be easy to move jobs to another team							

CHAPTER 24 - CLEANING TEMPLATES TO STREAMLINE YOUR OPERATIONS

These cleaning business email templates to provide notice to your customers. Templates make your job easy and ensure you are consistent with your company policies. Its key to use them at all times. Your office staff should also be able to follow these templates and use them on a daily basis.

Let's start...

Subject line: Cancellation Fee

xxxxxx,

We have cancelled your service for xxxxx. Please note that there is a cancellation fee of $xxxxx.

Please note that in the event that you need to reschedule, skip, or cancel your service, we ask that you provide us with a 2-business-days notice to avoid the cancellation fee of $50. Cancellations on the same day of service for any reason will be charged the 50% rate of service or $50, whichever is greater.

All cancellations must be made in writing via email to xxxxxxxx or by calling xxxxxxx.

Best Regards,

XXXXXXX

Cancellation Fee Waived Template #2

Subject line: Cancellation fee waived

Dear,

We have cancelled your service for xxxxx. We have waived your cancellation fee for this time.

Please note that in the event that you need to reschedule, skip, or cancel your service, we ask that you provide us with a 2-business-days notice to avoid the cancellation fee of $50. Cancellations on the same day of service for any reason will be charged the 50% rate of service or $50, whichever is greater.

All cancellations must be made in writing via email to xxxxxxxxx or by calling xxxxxxx.

Best Regards,

Subject line: cleaning service proposal follow up

xxxxxxx,

I have emailed you our Cleaning Service Proposal for your review, please let me know when would be a good time to follow up with you.

We look forward to a long lasting work relationship with you.

Best Regards,

XXXXXXX

Subject line: credit card decline notice

xxxxx,

Your credit card on file ending in XXXX has been declined.

We are sending you another credit card authorization form via Echosign/Adobe Document Cloud.

Let us know if you have any questions or concerns.

Warm Regards,

XXXXXXX

Subject line: expired credit card on file

XXXXX,

The credit card we have on file for you has expired. We have sent you a new form via EchoSign for you to fill out at your earliest convenience.

Best Regards,

XXXXXXX

Dear Client,

Your payment of $XXX.XX with the check number of XXX from <u>Bank Name</u> was returned to us.

Please see attached notice.

Please note that full payment is now due including a $35 charge for the bounced check fee. The total due is $XXX.XX.

You may call us to process a credit card over the phone or you can visit us online to make a payment via PayPal at http://www.tremendousmaid.com/make-a-payment/xxxxxxxxxxxxxx.

If you have any questions, please do not hesitate to contact us.

Warm Regards,

XXXXXX

Subject line: following up with today's cleaning service

Dear ,

xxxxxxxx visited your premises! Were you happy or could we have provided a better service?

If you are interested in receiving regular service at a flat rate quote we can send you a proposal. We offer weekly, biweekly, every 3 weeks and monthly service.

Warm Regards,

XXXXXXX

Subject line: regular service feedback request

Good ,

Here at xxxxxxxx we want to check to ensure you are receiving awesome service.

Are you happy? Or could we provide you with a better service?

Your feedback is very important to us.

Please Advise,

XXXXXXX

Subject line: pet feces notice

Dear ,

The maids have indicated on several occasions that they had to remove pet feces from the floors. Please know that our workers compensation insurance and OSHA guidelines do not allow us to request employees to remove feces without proper training and equipment. Our insurance does not cover us for any employees in the case that they get sick from being in touch with pet discharge while working for us; therefore, we communicate to the maids that they are not allowed to touch / remove / clean areas where it has been contaminated by human / pet discharge.

We would kindly request that any discharge be cleaned prior to our arrival. If discharge is found the maids have been requested not to touch the area.

Please let us know if you have any questions.

Thank you,

XXXXXXX

Checking All Keys Came back//Work Route Papers

1-Double check how many team worked the day before and ensure you got all keys (blue bag with a number, could be 1,2,3,4,5,6) The number is written with a black marker

2- Open the bag check if they have any checks, cash anything, if they do take it out and ensure you know why and how they have what they have inside the bulto.

3- Take the route sheet paper and keys.

4- Star looking for the house that said "KEY" in the work order if they do, ensure that key is back and if the key is just put it on the bowl.

5- Do step 4 with all bags.

NOTE - In case a key is missing

1- Check employees who were working in that team.

2-Call the employee to their cell and ask for the key that is missing.

3- If employees do not know, then ask Rosa.

4 - **If xxxxx Knows where the key** is then we are fine you just have to ensure Rosa gives you the key back so you can put it inside the bowl.

5- **If xxxxx does not have the key** then you have to report to manager xxxxxx.

6- If the key is really missing and is nowhere to be found, all the office team together has to think how to tell the client and take a decision on where provide client with a reimburse, etc.

7-Once all the keys are put the keys back in the safe at the end of the day.

CHAPTER 25 - STRATEGIC GROWTH THROUGH OPERATIONS AND BREAKING DOWN BIG GOALS INTO SMALL TASKS

After completing an operational audit, figure out a few areas of opportunity for improvement in order to achieve the growth forecasted in your growth plan. These challenges also could serve to help you increase customer satisfaction.

Identify 3 major processes that are to be scheduled for immediate improvement ---Sample Below.

#1 Customer Satisfaction / Communication

- Text via Google Voice
  - Text New Clients after Initial Cleaning to Get Feedback
  - Text Reg clients weekly and biweekly clients every 2 months to get feedback
  - Text Reg monthly clients every 3 months to get feedback
  - Text clients who complete an online quote request – We will first email and call them but if the clients do not answer within 2 hours, we will also text them.
- Email
  - Email clients who have completed their first cleanings and did not book regular service. If your target market prefers a call, make sure you pick up the phone and call the client to ask for feedback and also to ask them to book regular service. A good amount of our older (seniors) clients prefer phone calls instead of texting or emails.
  - Email inspection reports to commercial clients and regular residential clients
- In Person Meetings
  - Meetings on a quarterly basis for commercial clients is essential
  - Send email invites to confirm meetings

#2 Training Program

- **Attracting & Hiring 'the right' candidates**
  - Better Application (In English and Spanish)
  - Interviewing Process
    - Set of interviews
      - Application must be completely answered
      - Application must be done in-house (this will prevent to give out so many applications and to ensure that applicant is the person answering the questions
    - Scout Talent Test

- This test helps us determine if the person has the qualities we desire in people
  - Hiring Process
    - Background test completed
    - Reference check
    - Get paperwork ready for employee's signature

- **Training**
  - Orientation
    - Schedule first day of orientation to meet all staff members & watch first set of videos
    - 2nd Day question the learning from day 1 and show floor care & bathroom care training videos
  - Team Training
    - 3rd Day one-on-one training at our training units
  - Individual Training Sessions
    - Training with Lead Trainers
  - On the job training
    - One test day by 2nd week –Employee will clean by them without supervision. Once done the Training Manager will solicit his/her input.
    - Schedule 2nd day for employee to clean alone again and for Training Manager to give input after completion.
    - Once Trainee knows how to clean a house, the trainee then learns to clean a common space area in buildings such as hallways, elevator tracks, elevator panels, floors, etc.
    - Training will depend on the position hired for but all employees must learn to clean a house since it requires more attention to details

- **Performance Feedbacks**
  - 1 Week Check-In from Start Date
  - 2 Weeks Check-In from Start Date
  - 30 Days Check-In from Start Date
  - 60 Days Performance Feedback
  - 90 Days Performance Feedback
  - Every 4 months thereafter

- **Seminars**
  - Specific Workshops for all Team Members
    - Follow up Training to refresh Team Member's knowledge
    - Training on Customer Service
    - Training on Corporate Athlete

- Training Programs for Owners, Managers, Supervisors & Office Staff
  - Customer Service Programs
  - Employment Law / HR Topics
  - Corporate Athlete Program
  - Landmark Forum Program
  - Ongoing Programs to follow up on both Corporate Athlete & Landmark Forum

#3 Quality Assurance

- First Cleaning
- Regular Service Follow up
- Work Orders – Adding Value thru:
  - Auto Inspections Emailed to Clients
  - Allow clients to place work orders in the system
  - Place work orders in the system and email to client for their verifications
    - Meet with clients on a quarterly basis to gather feedback

Sample of a Journey Map that Needed Improvement Below: We used let the client find us, book the service and follow up with us. We needed to change this process immediately to ensure we make it easier for clients to book with us, give us input and sign up for regular service.

For example, the current journey map below indicates what steps are required to book service with us for the commercial and residential division:

Current Journey Map

We respond with Email if Quote requested via email & If via phone we request an onsite visitation

Rosa or Victoria provides On-site visitation

We return to office and complete a proposal and email it via echosign.com

Client finds us and Emails / Calls

We inspect the area monthly to ensure consistency

If clients agree we schedule the first cleaning

Inspect facility on a monthly basis

Journey Map Improved

Actively search for potential clients via print media, networking events, and continuous email marketing: Consistent

Follow Up by Wed (Every Wed from 10am to 2pm – leave message if there is not answer

Request meeting to review potential working relationship –and offer a proposal during the meeting for their review – proposal valid for 45 days only otherwise we need to

If proposal is requested: Draft, Email and Follow up within 2 days and offer to meet in person to review

Once we are chosen – provide first visit and schedule touch points

Schedule on-site inspections and ensure clients receive copy of

When meeting on a bimonthly basis – ensure we take the client out for lunch or dinner or a sports - these are not cleaning meetings – these meetings are

For the residential division, we also had changed several processes to ensure we continued to grow in that area.

One of the major changes is that all one-time cleaning clients will receive a text message via Google voice to ask for quick feedback. If the client is happy, we will offer a date and time for a second cleaning. If the client is not happy, we call immediately to find out what went wrong and if we can dispatch a team to return and clean the areas in questions. Immediately after, we will follow up with the client again to ensure 100% happiness.

Immediate Action Steps:

- Create a template for each text message so the office staff has a few options for sending the text messages based if it's a new client, existing client, message if client is happy or upset, etc. Text messages must be fun but professional.

- Office assistant must call everyone that sends an email for both residential and commercial clients. Currently we simply respond back with an email. Starting immediately, we will reply with an email and call within 1 hour if we do not get a response back.

- Set up an auto remainder to do 30, 60, 90 and every 6 months performance feedback with each team member. Automating the schedule through our scheduling manager program and Google calendar would help us ensure that performance reviews are always consistent. This will help us determining which employees need further training in specific areas to ensure the best customer service possible.

- Send email invites to secure on site visitations via Google Calendar. We will offer meeting online via Webex to clients that prefer meeting online instead of in person. This will appear to the younger managers and also help to reduce travel time and travel expense (gas, tolls, and parking)

- Purchase of new equipment to help increase efficiency is necessary:

  - Auto Scrubbers to scrub floors in a fast timely manner

o Auto Extractors that can be pushed and pulled to minimize time travel from filling up tanks, pushing and pulling the wand and to make it easy for women to utilize without the need of a man.
o Wide area vacuums to decrease vacuum time in large buildings

CHAPTER 26 – WHAT TO ENSURE CLEANERS HAVE BEFORE LEAVING FOR THE FIRST CLEANING

Ensure all the cars have all the supplies needed for the day

- ✓ 1 bottle of Ajax or similar product,
- ✓ 1 Bottle of dishwashing soap,
- ✓ 1 bottle of mildew remover
- ✓ 1 bottle of Neutral Bathroom Cleaner
- ✓ 1 Bottle of Stain Steel Cleaner
- ✓ 1 bottle of Degreaser,
- ✓ 1 Bottle of air freshener,
- ✓ 1 Bottle of Glass Cleaner
- ✓ 1 Roll of Trash Bags,
- ✓ 1-2 Yellow Cleaning Rags,
- ✓ 1 Regular Vacuum, and 1 Backpack Vacuum
- ✓ 1 Feather Dusters, Cleaning Basket,
- ✓ 2 Steps Ladder.
- ✓ 1 Broom
- ✓ 1 Bag of 45 little cleaning rugs (mostly white) and 8 big rugs to be used as mop
- ✓ 1-2 Dish scrubbers (ensure all cars have this inside, if not put them in or have the supplies ready for the maids to put it inside of the car)

Receiving employees for their shifts
1. Read all note from all the jobs employees are to perform during the day.
2. Once employees are here ensure they come in on time -take attendance.

3. Once all members of each team are here do a little reunion & give them instructions for each specific cleaning job.
4. Tell them to check the car to see if they have everything they need
5. Check each other work performance.
6. Make sure they leave with all the keys for the right houses on their work orders

CHAPTER 27 - WHAT TO LOOK FOR WHEN INSPECTING RESIDENTIAL HOUSE SAMPLE

1- Check bathroom is properly cleaned

- ✓ No stains on tiles wall
- ✓ No stains inside the toilet or sink
- ✓ Bathtub well scrubbed
- ✓ Floor mopped really well

2- Check Kitchen is properly Cleaned

- ✓ Counter properly whipped
- ✓ If oven/fridge are done ensure they are properly cleaned and have no stains
- ✓ Mops are well mopped
- ✓ Nothing is broken or damaged

3- Bedroom

- ✓ All bed are properly made
- ✓ Trash taken out
- ✓ Floor properly mopped if rugs/ properly vacuumed
- ✓ Dust

4- Living room

- ✓ Dusted properly
- ✓ Vacuum & Mopped really well
- ✓ Ensure nothing is broken or damaged

CHAPTER 28 - PROCESS TO RECEIVE CLEANERS PAPERWORK AT END OF EACH SHIFT

 I hope they have been extremely valuable - make sure to subscribe to my channel here and visit my website at **TREMENDOUSLIFE.COM** and subscribe to my newsletter

Checking All Keys Came back//Work Route Papers

1-Double check how many team worked the day before and ensure you got all keys (blue bag with a number, could be 1,2,3,4,5,6) The number is written with a black marker

2- Open the bag check if they have any checks, cash anything, if they do take it out and ensure you know why and how they have what they have inside the bulto.

3- Take the route sheet paper and keys.

4- Star looking for the house that said "KEY" in the work order if they do, ensure that key is back and if the key is just put it on the bowl.

5- Do step 4 with all bags.

NOTE - In case a key is missing

1- Check employees who were working in that team.

2-Call the employee to their cell and ask for the key that is missing.

3- If employees do not know, then ask Rosa.

4 - **If xxxxx Knows where the key** is then we are fine you just have to ensure Rosa gives you the key back so you can put it inside the bowl.

5- **If xxxxx does not have the key** then you have to report to manager xxxxxx.

6- If the key is really missing and is nowhere to be found, all the office team together has to think how to tell the client and take a decision on where provide client with a reimburse, etc.

7-Once all the keys are put the keys back in the safe at the end of the day.

CHAPTER 29 - NEW COMMERCIAL CLIENTS BUSINESS FORM

*Any new client must sign this form prior to 1st cleaning and all forms MUST have a valid EIN / Tax Id # --no exceptions.

1) xxxx to send form to new one time clients seeking service of any client —These are clients who have <u>not</u> requested an on-site—seeking one time carpet cleaning, floor cleaning, one deep cleaning based on hourly rate etc. If a one time client requests a proposal, xxxxx will write up proposal and send the form with the proposal. xxxxx has to follow up with client to ensure form is filled 100%.

2) If Reg client seeking service then xxxx will send form with proposal

3) xxxx will check tax id # to confirm match

4) Completed form to be placed inside banner located in xxxxx's office for future reference

5) If a past due invoice then xxxxxx to address based on current accounts receivables policies.

6) If invoice is past due over <u>45 days</u> xxxx to send official letter to business owner to address the late payment xxx to discuss letter with xxx and (xx if needed).

Thank you!

xxxxxx

New Account / Credit Application Form – For new clients who prefer to be invoiced

*Incomplete application may not be processed and cleaning service will not be scheduled

Physical Business Address for Billing Purposes:	Cleaning Service to be provided at following address (if different from the bill to address):
Corporation Name:	Corporation Name:
Tax ID (EIN #):	Address Street:
Trade Name (d/b/a):	City:
Address Street:	State:
City: State: Zip:	Zip:
Phone No:	Main Contact:
Fax No:	Main Contact Tel #:
Email Address:	

Business Facts:

___Proprietorship __ Partnership ___Corporation ___Other:_____

Accounting Information
Accounts Payable Contact:
Tel Phone:

Email Address:
Address if different than billing address:
Phone No:
Fax No:
Email Address:

Terms & Conditions:

Parties hereby agree that all services provided are subject to the following terms and conditions.

1. Company xyz normally expect payments the same day service/s is/are rendered. In the event that you need a different payment term please choose so here: ___**Net 7** ___**Net 14** ___**Net 30**

2. Accounts that are considered delinquent will be charge an additional $30, collection fees (payable by customer), and/ or cancellation of service may result if delinquency persist. Additionally, a 5% interest charge will apply on a monthly basis for any amount owed.

3. Any invoices pending after 30 days from service rendered are considered past due and delinquent.

4. Late payments that have to be turned over to company xyz attorney or collection agency will also be subject to additional charges to cover the additional legal expenses.

Customer Signature:_____ Date:_____

Printed Name: _____

CHAPTER 30 - BLOG WRITING GUIDELINES

Blogs for early stage leads must help to educate them to do their jobs better. Blogs must be build a relationship ---this is not the time to sell but to engage, educate, make their jobs easier. Blogs should be focused on how to identify a problem, how to articles, short video clips, post on awards, why we do what we do –see ted talk

http://www.ted.com/talks/simon_sinek_how_great_leaders_inspire_action?language=en

Mid stage blogs: how to solve the pain points of our potential customers, case studies, eguides, videos, provide more info on how we do what we do

Late stage blogs: leads know what they have to fix so our job is to help fix their problems as it relates to our services, blog post comparing bbc with other vendors, buyer guides, sample RFPs, etc.

Blogs to upsell, cross-sell, to maintain current clients engaged and our services as top of mind (this is something needed), and also to revive cold dead leads.
Use blogs / emails in CRM for sales and support such as asking to keep current invoice personnel updated, checking in every 2 months to check on client satisfaction / feedback on how to do our jobs even better to better service our clients!
Lost deal nurturing program campaign – check every 3 months with loss deals contacts!

Goal of social media / blogs:

- ✓ Establish credibility and authority –we want to be a leader in the commercial cleaning in the boston area
- ✓ Tell our story –the why we do what we do, how we do and what is it that we do
- ✓ Inspire customers to love us, trust us, admire us
- ✓ Be human – speak human

Potential schedule:

- ✓ Daily linkedin , twitter, and facebook updates
- ✓ Weekly 1-2 blogs for xyz
- ✓ Monthly:
  - Once per month a slideshare presentation
  - Once per month a short video
- ✓ Quarterly:
  - Every 3 months a longer video –a bit on the professionally done

- Eguide /whitepaper / case study – 'concept driven' etc

Sample:

What is an office cleaner doing on linked in /or twitter

The right way to get the right quote from your vendors / contractors / cleaning company provider

What cleaning has to do with DREAMING

Note:

Landing pages for FB, Twitter, Linkedin and Invoices

LOGO

Logo of diff awards

Home Cleaning Proposal

Ms. First Name, Last Name

ADDRESS

CITY, STATE

Office: (xxxxxxxx) | Fax: (xxxxxxxx)

WEB: www.xxxxxxxxxx.com

EMAIL: xxxxxxxxxxxxx

Office Address:
Full Address

Client name

Full Address

Dear Ms. Xxxxx,

As promised, here is the proposal so you know what to expect when working with xxxxxxx.

Here are top 3 benefits when you work with us:

Please do not hesitate to contact us if you have any questions or concerns.

We appreciate your consideration of our services and look forward to continuing working with you.

Sincerely,

Manager's Name

Title

Main Direct #

Using Company's Name Chemicals & Equipment

We provide all the supplies and equipment necessary, with these exceptions.

Toilet Brushes / Kitchen Sponge / Trash Can Liners & specialty cleaners.

xxxxxxx

Specialty Cleaners could be but are not limited to:

We ask that you supply specific cleaners for surfaces that require manufacturer's recommended products such as stone counters, marble floors and certain types of wood floors.

Customer Guidelines

Entry to your home

We offer 3 entry options to choose from:

1. *The client may opt to be home to allow access to their home the day of the service.*

   xxxxxx cannot guarantee the exact arrival times so the client must be home between the time scheduled to let the cleaner into the home. If no one is home or our cleaners are turned away for any reason there would be a lockout fee of 50% of your cleaning rate (Minimum of $50)

2. *The client provides a key, garage door opener or code to gain access to the home.*

   Keys will be placed in a secure safe at xxxxxxx's office. The cleaner or team will be issued a key the day of your scheduled service to gain access to the home. The key will be signed out by the cleaner or team and signed in after each scheduled service and placed back in the safe. The keys are not marked with any of your personal information in case they are lost. In the event the code given is not correct and cleaners cannot gain access to the home the client is responsible for the lock out of 50% of the total rate will be charged for that service.

3. *The client can purchase a lock box to place a key inside and provide xxxxxxxx with the pass code.*

In the event for any reason the key is not in the lock box or the code does not work when the cleaners arrive to clean home; the client is responsible for the lock out and a cancellation fee of 50% of the total rate would be charged for that service.

NOTE: In the event the client chooses to leave a door unlocked or place a key under a mat or any other unsecured place for the cleaners to gain entry into the home, the client releases xxxxxxxxxx form any issues prior or after we have cleaned the unit.

Schedule changes & cancellation of service:

In the event that you reschedule, skip, add or cancel your service, we ask that you give a 48-hour notice. Without a 48-hour notice you will be charged 50% of your cleaning. Cancellations on the same day of service for any reason will be charged the full rate of service. All cancellations must be made in writing via email to xxxxxxxxxx.

NOTE: If cancellations becomes a pattern, it will cause the rate for your next cleaning to increase to the next level….explain what that means and give them an example

Payment

Payment is due in full the day of the service.

XXXXXXXXX accepts cash, checks, Visa, MasterCard and Discover as well as Paypal. Checks returned from client's bank will be assessed an additional fee of $40.

Special requests

Any services requiring extra labor, supplies and/or equipment will be billed additionally for these services. Any services not normally included in the cleaning package that the client selected will be an added charge unless it is noted in the client's service agreement.

Breakage

What would you cover and not cover?

Our xxxxxx guarantee

Here include your guarantee and how long until they can report issues with service so you can dispatch cleaners again.

Specifications: General/ Regular Cleaning

Kitchen	Notes:
Refrigerator – clean outside and top – if excesive decorative items or papers – only wipe were possible without damaging papers	
Clean stove-top and range hood	
Microwave – clean outside/inside	
Clean and disinfect countertops and back splash	
Clean/disinfect/polish sinks and faucets	
Vacuum floor rugs	
Baseboards throughout & windowsills	
Empty trash	
Dust ceiling corners	
Vacuum floor and Mop floors	
Damp mop hard floor	
Wipe Outside cabinets	
Hand wipe light fixtures/disinfect switches (if Light fixtures must be acc. w 2 step ladder	**Must be accessible with a 2step ladder**

Bathroom   Notes:

Clean and disinfect tubs and shower	
Clean mirrors	
Clean exterior of vanities	
Clean/disinfect/polish sink and faucets	
Clean/disinfect countertops	
Clean and disinfect toilets	
Clean and disinfect floors	
Hand wipe baseboards	
Dust light fixtures (outside only) disinfect switches	
Clean and disinfect towel bars	
Empty trash	

Common Rooms & Bedroom

Vacuum/dust mop wood floors	
Dust light fixtures and disinfect switches	
Wipe base boards	
Dust ceiling corners	
Clean window glass panels on inside only	
Wipe furniture and dust picture frames	
Vacuum furniture and dust cushions (underneath area as well)	

TV and general electrodomestics– only dust with duster	
Dust blinds with duster or damped cleaning	

*Please leave bed linen out for the maids if you would like for the bed linen to be replaced.

The following services can be provided for an additional charge:

Service	Price	Notes:
Kitchen cabinets (inside)	$xxx	
Oven inside	$xx	
Refrigerator	$xx	
Blind cleaning	$xxx per hr	
Walls	$xxx per hr	

Payment Agreement

I understand that in the event that I cancel my scheduled service without giving 48-hour notice I will be charged $50.00.

- I understand that there is a 50% lock-out fee from the full rate of service. Lock out fee means that the maids were scheduled, dispatched to clean your home but they didn't obtain access to the unit.

- I understand t hat payment is due in full on the day of service.
- I understand that xxxxxx accepts cash, checks, Visa, MasterCard and Discover.
- I understand that any NSF (insufficient funds) checks will be resolved by charging my back up credit card on file for the past due amount along with any NSF fees.
- I understand that XXXXXXXXX reserves the right to raise prices at anytime and will give me an advanced notice of any price increases.
- I understand that special requests are to be made 24 hours in advance and that there will be additional charges if those requests are not included in the cleaning package I selected.

Insurance Policy Information

Commercial General Liability Coverage / Workers Comp

Service Agreement

Ms. First Name, Last Name,

The biweekly rate for your unit is $xxx per visit.

Ongoing service that will be performed is based on the included list of Cleaning Specifications.

- **I understand that in the event that I cancel my scheduled service without giving 48-hour notice I will be charged $50.00.**
- **I understand that there is a lock-out fee of 50% from the full rate of service.**

Note: XXXXXXXXX hourly rate is $xx for two cleaners or $xxx with 3 maids. If hiring us to work on an hourly basis is more valuable for you, please inform us immediately.

- Cleaning chemicals and equipment to perform this service will be supplied by XXXXXXXXX.

- In the event that this Agreement proves unsatisfactory, a 48-Hour notice by writing via email to info@xxxx.com by either party may terminate it. If client terminates without 48-Hour notice and the cleaners arrive as scheduled, client will be billed for that service.

- Payment Terms: Payment is due in full on day of service.

- Additional services requested that are not included on the Cleaning Specifications list will be invoiced separately.

This is not a binding contract. Either client or XXXXXXXXX can cancel this agreement with 5 business days advance notice from the next scheduled service.

Customer Signature: _____

Date: _____

Other Tel: _____ Mobile: _____

Email: _____

FINAL MESSAGE...

 I hope this manual have been extremely valuable - make sure to subscribe to visit my website at **TREMENDOUSLIFE.COM** and subscribe to my newsletter. My email is info@tremendouslife.com

I hope to see you on the video course called The 6 Figure Cleaning Business Master Class.

Congratulations on your cleaning business journey!

Made in United States
Troutdale, OR
09/03/2023

12595522R00092